BEFORE YOU START READING,
DOWNLOAD YOUR FREE BONUSES!

Scan the QR-code & Access
all the Resources for FREE!

SCAN ME

The Self-Sufficient Living Cheat Sheet

10 Simple Steps to Become More Self-Sufficient in 1 Hour or Less

How to restore balance to the environment around you… even if you live in a tiny apartment in the city.

Discover:

- **How to increase your income** by selling "useless" household items
- The environmentally friendly way to replace your car — invest in THIS special vehicle to **eliminate your carbon footprint**
- The secret ingredient to **turning your backyard into a thriving garden**
- 17+ different types of food scraps and 'waste' that you can use to feed your garden
- How to drastically **cut down on food waste** without eating less
- 4 natural products you can use to make your own eco-friendly cleaning supplies
- The simple alternative to 'consumerism' — the age-old method for **getting what you need without paying money for it**
- The 9 fundamental items you need to create a self-sufficient first-aid kit
- One of the top skills that most people are afraid of learning — and how you can master it effortlessly
- 3 essential tips for **gaining financial independence**

The Prepper Emergency Preparedness & Survival Checklist:
10 Easy Things You Can Do Right Now to Ready Your Family
& Home for Any Life-Threatening Catastrophe

**Natural disasters demolish everything in their path, but
your peace of mind and sense of safety don't have to be
among them. Here's what you need to know…**

- Why having an emergency plan in place is so crucial
  and how it will help to keep your family safe
- How to stockpile emergency supplies intelligently and
  why you shouldn't overdo it
- How to store and conserve water so that you know
  you'll have enough to last you through the crisis
- A powerful 3-step guide to ensuring financial
  preparedness, no matter what happens
- A step-by-step guide to maximizing your storage space,
  so you and your family can have exactly what you need
  ready and available at all times
- Why knowing the hazards of your home ahead of time
  could save a life and how to steer clear of these in case
  of an emergency
- Everything you need to know for creating a successful
  evacuation plan, should the worst happen and you
  need to flee safely

101 Recipes, Tips, Crafts, DIY Projects and More for a Beautiful Low Waste Life
Reduce Your Carbon Footprint and Make Earth-Friendly Living Fun With This Comprehensive Guide

Practical, easy ways to improve your personal health and habits while contributing to a brighter future for yourself and the planet

Discover:
- **Simple customizable recipes for creating your own food, home garden, and skincare products**
- The tools you need for each project to successfully achieve sustainable living
- Step-by-step instructions for life-enhancing skills from preserving food to raising your own animals and forging for wild berries
- **Realistic life changes that reduce your carbon-footprint while saving you money**
- Sustainable crafts that don't require any previous knowledge or expertise
- Self-care that extends beyond the individual and positively impacts the environment
- **Essential tips on how to take back control of your life -- become self-sustained and independent**

First Aid Fundamentals
A Step-By-Step Illustrated Guide to the Top 10 Essential First Aid Procedures Everyone Should Know

Discover:

- **What you should do to keep this type of animal attack from turning into a fatal allergic reaction**
- Why sprains are more than just minor injuries, and how you can keep them from getting worse
- **How to make the best use of your environment in critical situations**
- The difference between second- and third-degree burns, and what you should do when either one happens
- Why treating a burn with ice can actually cause more damage to your skin
- When to use heat to treat an injury, and when you should use something cold
- **How to determine the severity of frostbite**, and what you should do in specific cases
- Why knowing this popular disco song could help you save a life
- The key first aid skill that everyone should know — **make sure you learn THIS technique the right way**

Food Preservation Starter Kit
10 Beginner-Friendly Ways to Preserve Food at Home |
Including Instructional Illustrations and Simple Directions

Grocery store prices are skyrocketing! It's time for a self-sustaining lifestyle.

Discover:

- **10 incredibly effective and easy ways to preserve your food for a self-sustaining lifestyle**
- The art of canning and the many different ways you can preserve food efficiently without any prior experience
- A glorious trip down memory lane to learn the historical methods of preservation passed down from one generation to the next
- **How to make your own pickled goods**: enjoy the tanginess straight from your kitchen
- Detailed illustrations and directions so you won't feel lost in the preservation process
- The health benefits of dehydrating your food and how fermentation can be **the key to a self-sufficient life**
- **The secrets to living a processed-free life** and saving Mother Earth all at the same time

Get all the resources for FREE by scanning the QR-Code below:

SCAN ME

Raising Goats For Beginners 2022-2023

A Step-By-Step Guide to Raising Happy, Healthy Goats For Milk, Cheese, Meat, Fiber, and More With the Most Up-To-Date Information

Small Footprint Press

Table of Contents

Introduction

"Until one has loved an animal, a part of one's soul remains unawakened."

— Anatole France

It is often said that you can take the boy from the farm, but not the farm out of the boy. Many of us have an inborn sense of peace when we look out at our acreage and watch our animals at play, eating, and experiencing the joy of just being out in the sunshine and living in the moment.

Whether you are just head over heels in love with animals or merely wanting your life to slow down so that you can enjoy those simpler moments, the appeal of your own patch of land and many adoring eyes may be just the lifestyle choice you need.

The return to rural roots is devoid of cabs on every corner, elevated trains, or quick pizza delivery. You will be reliant on your own resources to get things done and plan for problematic seasons that bring with them weather challenges. You might never realize how good you are with tools until you have to repair your own tractor, but there are usually some friendly neighbors that can often lend a helping hand.

Rural areas might have fewer banks, dry cleaners, mechanics, babysitters, or even grocery store choices. However, you will become proficient at lists when you go to town.

While it may be an adjustment to relocate and become a member of the simpler country mindset and way of life, there are some outstanding benefits to be gained. More people realize that there are many advantages from living the country life that they never considered before.

For example, our recent pandemic has proven to us all that living in a heavily populated area can be a health risk.

When you live out in the rural areas, life tends to slow down, and you learn to appreciate all those little things you didn't realize were being taken for granted. Your air quality is better, and the rural setting is by far more healthy than living in any large downtown city. By switching to rural areas, you will find that you are able to live in a healthier way, resulting in far fewer health issues.

After moving to your little piece of heaven, you may discover that your brain changes the way it thinks, and you prioritize things differently. When you live in a more crowded area, you may find yourself over-stimulated and filled with anxiety. Rural living provides a more peaceful setting and every morning, you can still enjoy your cup of coffee, but instead of looking out of your apartment window and being flooded with honking horns of traffic, you can now look out upon animals enjoying their breakfast, playing, or even trusting to take a morning snooze in a sunbeam.

Tranquility has no price tag.

So, what animals appeal to you? If you are wondering about raising goats, look no further! There are many reasons to raise goats other than they can be fun to watch. They can provide you with meat, dairy, fiber, or entertainment. This book will discuss the benefits, tips, and pitfalls to avoid while raising your very own herd of goats.

You may have lived your entire life in the USA, and not know that goat meat is the most popular meat in the world. It is very high in protein, and goat meat is growing in demand annually. If you cannot face the goat meat industry, that's okay because there are plenty of other things you can do with them, including raising your goats for milk and by-products like cheese and yogurt. Were you aware that you can raise brush-eating goats? Believe it or not, there is always someone wanting to lease a herd of goats in order to clear brush and weeds from their fields.

Our goal here at Small Footprint Press is to help you sustainably survive and thrive while ensuring together that the world is a better place for future generations to come.

Born out of frustration with the planet's current state, we want to raise awareness about how we all affect the world we live in and what you can do yourself & collectively to make a real difference.

We know how important it is to start giving back to the earth and how true happiness can come from living sustainably. Furthermore, having your own backyard goats is an incredible way to put your worries to rest and become more self-reliant.

That's why we've taken the time to make sure that you feel safe and empowered in your own journey to sustainability. As the world gets more confusing each day, we are determined to keep life simple and ensure that everyone has the ability to survive off their own, homegrown food, no matter what situation they may face.

If you have a love for all things outdoors and truly want to make the Earth a better place, then we can help guide you through all the small chores associated with the raising of goats. Our planet needs people just like you who want to see our world improve, and learn to be the best version of ourselves. If you can make a living doing something that you love, what is stopping you?

Chapter 1:

Are You Properly Prepared?

Depending upon where you currently live, there can be some laws in place that govern the keeping, raising, transport, and welfare of any animal kept on your property. Since these rules will vary greatly, the first thing that you should do is some homework on what animals are allowed on your property and how many animals might be mandated per acre. The last thing any animal lover wants to do is get some critters, get attached to them, and then have to give up our dream before we even get started. Be prepared to do plenty of research before buying your first animal.

According to the Animal Welfare Act (2006), anyone owning an animal has a legal responsibility to fulfill the five basic welfare needs of their pets and farm animals. These needs are stated below:

- A proper diet
- A suitable shelter in which to live
- Any animal requiring a need to be kept separate from other animals should have those facilities available for them
- Any animal must be allowed to express normal behavior

- Any animal must be provided protection from and treatment for any illness and injury

Since goats are categorized as a farm animal species, all owners of goats must comply with some extra laws. There are laws that include, but are not limited to:

- The registration of the land on which you are keeping goats
- The way the goats are identified
- The transportation of goats
- The meticulous record-keeping of medicines and health issues

You should contact your local government officials regarding any law they may have regarding the housing of goats on your property and study your legal obligations.

- Always check any zoning or ordinances that might stand in your way. I know you have been daydreaming about goats and probably counting them as you fall asleep, but you first need to determine if your property is zoned for them. Many cities or towns will not allow goats and since it is probably not a largely requested topic, they may not be sure at first. Whoever you ask, preferably in writing, will most likely need to check out any zoning codes or municipal ordinances regarding the legalities of goat keeping on your property. It may be difficult to traverse some of the definitions when it comes to raising goats on your property. There are even codes that prohibit agriculture as a 'gainful business,' so you may be allowed to raise them for personal use, but cannot make them your livelihood. By checking town ordinances and bylaws, you should be able to determine if your goats would be welcome in the community or banned and labeled as a 'nuisance animal.' We all know that goats can be impressive escape artists and should they get into your neighbor's garden, there could be some damage that your insurance will need to cover. Always be prepared.

- Even if your city or town allows the ownership of goats, don't make the mistake of not checking your homeowner's association (HOA) should your property fall under their rules.
- Know all the rules. Even if you are lucky enough to live in an area that permits goats, there still might be some rules that you may have to follow. Some of these exceptions may include:
  - Goats must be dehorned
  - Male goats must be neutered
  - Size might make a difference - perhaps your area may only allow miniature goats such as Pygmy or Dwarf
  - There might be a stipulation on how many goats you are allowed on your property. It might surprise you that

there can be no less than and no more than rule in place when it comes to how many goats you are allowed.

- ○ While your goats must be kept in a shelter, there may be specific design, size, and placement requirements that you must follow.

- ○ There could be a rule in place about your shelter having direct access to an outdoor fenced-in enclosure. In addition, there could be specific designs, area, height, and other requirements regarding your pasture and fencing.

- Goats leave their droppings all over, and there will likely be rules about the removal and disposal of their waste so that it will not contaminate land, water, or cause potential health issues.

- Only personal consumption or benefits from goat-originated products may be allowed, in other words, no sales. This might be a problem if you wanted a goat-based business!

Just because this might fit your plans for today, don't overlook your future dreams. Anytime you commit to ownership of an animal, that is a responsibility, and you should keep in mind the lifespan of any animals you share your home and life with. Should you have an upcoming move in your future, the next property will also need to allow your goats. Before you sign on the dotted line for your new property, you should know all the rules and restrictions. If you have plans to add to your herd, make sure that your rules will allow you to add to your group without having to shop for another property if you want to expand.

Lastly, just because your area doesn't allow goats now, there are always steps you can go through to change your local laws in your favor.

- Do your breed research because it might surprise you to learn that some goats are noisier than others! If you rack up some noise citations, or your new neighbors complain of the smell or an overabundance of flies, this can reward you with some grief.
- As I mentioned above, make sure that your liability insurance covers property damage caused by your new goat herd. It seems that expensive landscaping is the tastiest morsel to a goat on the lam (if you will pardon the pun).

Size May Matter

Goats come in all shapes and sizes, and they also can differ in purpose and temperament. You may or may not be limited to smaller goats due to property restrictions, but now comes the hardest part; which goats are right for you? You are going to have to do your research before deciding on which goats are for you.

Full Size Vs Mini Goats

If you are looking for milking goats, many swear that the full-size goats are not only easier to milk, but they produce a higher yield. While this is true, larger goats can also be more difficult to handle. Despite the fact that some breeds can be more ornery than others, the amount of space you have available and the amount of milk you will need can be more of a deciding factor when deciding on a breed than their temperament.

Being a new goat keeper can sometimes seem difficult when it comes right down to making critical decisions, and that's why we will try to detail some scenarios below:

1. If what you desire is no-nonsense milk, and you want a larger yield, but have an acre or less, then you might want to look at a couple of full-sized does. One full-sized doe of virtually any breed will produce a gallon of milk each day. Two

such does, will bring you 14 gallons of milk each week. This is an estimated amount, and you may experience a bit more or a bit less but what are your plans for this quantity of milk each week? Maybe you have a large family that consumes a lot of milk, but if you don't, are you planning to sell it? Maybe you are planning to get into cheese making? Remember, that with full-sized goats, you will need higher and sturdier fencing because they can be very destructive. It's probably a good rule of thumb to plan on more food and more supplies in general.

2. This option will be very similar to number one, except you will want to proceed with two Nigerian Dwarf does. Instead of worrying about what you are going to do with 14 gallons each week, this pair of goats will provide you with half that amount, or 7 gallons a week. This provides you with a reasonable amount of milk each week, and the size of these goats will not impact your feed bill as much as the full-size animals.

3. Looking for something midway between these choices? Then perhaps you should look at two goats from a mini breed. Pygmies and Nigerian Dwarfs are considered mini breeds, and any crosses with Nigerians are still considered a mini breed. Any doe from these breeds or crosses typically produces just over a ½ a gallon

each day. The amount of milk can vary because of the animal being crossbred.

Often it just takes some experience for people to learn how to plan ahead based upon individual milk production. Once you are blessed with extra milk, you end up finding ways to use it up. Products like soaps and cheese use a considerable amount of milk. You may not be ready to start production on these products just yet. However, if it is something you are thinking about for the future, instead of adding more goats to your start-up, then the full-sized goats may be your better solution.

We find that your choices are going to be made not only on the characteristics of the individual animals, but also on your ultimate goals. If you have never owned goats before, the Nigerian Dwarfs may seem like a better choice to get started. They are smaller and often easier to handle than their larger counterparts. Nigerian dwarfs are known for their great temperament and could be a great choice for a new goat herd owner.

Another reason this breed appeals to the majority of people is that their milk has the most butterfat ratio than other breeds. (This generally means it is tastier!)

Then there is the choice of keeping a buck. One smaller Nigerian buck can be easier to handle and contain versus a full-sized one.

Goat Dynamics

Goat herds can be found in a myriad of places, and not just on fertile dairy fields that we picture in Wisconsin or Minnesota. Goats are geographically the most widespread species of livestock. These animals are adaptable and herds litter the globe, from the deserts of Africa to the frigid mountainous regions of Siberia. According to Carol Amundson (2020), some studies show amid the world goat population, there is only a variation of about 10% in DNA results.

People have various reasons for choosing to raise goats. While one might just want to have some cute pets around to strut their stuff throughout their pasture, others may want to create a lifestyle of raising goats for sustainable income or self-sufficiency. Either way, if you are new to raising goats, there are certain behaviors that you will need to understand. You may have always thought of goats as mere farm animals or a favorite in the circle of chosen petting zoos. However, they also can prove to be good pets. If you are lucky enough to have a herd, you will find by watching them that there are a few key players that call the shots among your group:

- Herd Queen. There's one in every herd, and this one is the dominant female. No, she doesn't parade around with a crown on her head, but she might as well because this queen leads the way, deciding when the herd can go out to the pasture. She will always have the best sleeping spot, most likely right in front of the feeders. Should she be a dairy goat, she will be the first to be milked. Heaven help any goat that tries to change the pecking order because the herd queen will put them in their place quickly.

Any offspring of the herd queen are treated like royalty and are included in the queen's favorite eating spots. Like any mother, the queen will defend them if any other goats try to push them out of the way.

The herd queen does have some responsibilities because she is the first one to test any new plants and determine if it is beneficial for the rest of the herd. She is also considered the first line of defense against predators and will remain in her position until she dies or becomes old and sick. At this time, another doe will fight and take over the head position.

- Head Buck. Traditionally, this position is held by the biggest, strongest, and oldest buck. This buck will retain his position until he dies or a younger buck from the herd challenges him and wins.

Any intact males within your herd will have a certain smell. How shall we put this delicately? They stink! Your nose may find it very offensive, not to mention anyone who visits your farm that knows nothing about goats.

You may have already been aware that bucks will smell bad, but you may not know why. The musky odor that is specific to bucks comes from a combination of their urine and their scent glands. Just in case you need to know, these scent glands are located near their horns.

Bucks are a bit disturbing with their hygiene habits, choosing to spray their urine in their beards, chest, face, and front legs more than normal during the time of rut. You may find this surprising, but does seem to find the odor irresistible.

When you find out how badly they stink, you may decide to opt for artificial insemination or just lease a buck to breed your does and then send him packing for home.

- Kids. The survival and the increase of your herd depend upon the kids. If you want to perpetuate a thriving dairy, you will need kids in order for your does to provide you with milk. By raising kids, you will fortify your herd's bloodline and be able to replace aging animals.

According to legend, we even have goats to thank for the discovery of coffee. To this day, some goat owners will use it to stimulate labor.

No herd is complete without the antics of young kids. While most does are excellent mothers, there may be times when you will need to step in and lend a hand. Situations that may require extra support include:

  o In very cold or wet weather when the kid is born, they tend to lose body energy and heat quickly. As a result, they may become weakened and you will need to step in to ensure their survival.

○ Maiden does may lack experience in the care of their newborn kids. The last thing you want to experience is a mother abandoning their kids, but it does happen, and you will need to take action immediately. If you have a doe with poor mothering abilities, you may want to cull them from your herd. Bottle feeding colostrum to kids may be necessary if they are not suckling.

○ If your doe starts showing signs of poor health just prior to birth, they may show a lack of interest in their newborns. They may also not be able to produce enough colostrum and milk that is required by their new kids.

○ Multiple births can prove difficult even for the most experienced does. When three or more kids are born, there may not be enough nourishment for all of them.

○ Weak newborns may not be able to suckle or stand on their own.

○ Your kidding area should be well protected from predators so that your newborns are not killed or injured by predators and the mothers are not stressed out.

○ Overcrowding can cause aggressive animals in a herd to attack newborn kids, which is why you should have a separate kidding area.

If you are contemplating owning goats, you need to know that they are herd animals and will require at least one partner of the same species. In addition, they will need at bare minimum a large yard in which to roam and embrace their typical goat behavior. They will need and desire the same amount of attention that you would give to any pet or livestock animal you own. Just as any other pack or herd animal, you should never openly play favorites because, believe it or not, goats do become jealous and could display some aggression if not receiving their fair share of affection.

While you observe your herd interact, you will be intrigued by the way they communicate with each other. Here are some behaviors you will eventually become accustomed to:

- Biting: Goats will often communicate by biting.

- Butting: Why do goats butt? They tend to use their butting ability to bully others for a number of reasons. They may be establishing their place in the herd, pushing others out of their way, as a form of play, or to fight.

Butting is a very persuasive reason to dehorn your goats and, in addition, you should never keep horned and dehorned goats together because this is an open invitation for one of them to get seriously injured.

You will see an increase in biting and butting when a new herd member is introduced. Because of the newcomer, lower-status herd members are the first to initiate the fighting, primarily because they want to maintain or raise their position within the herd.

- Rut: What is a goat buck in rut? Rut, put simply, is a period of time in a buck's life when they experience a surge of hormones and become ready to breed. A buck can be ready to breed throughout the year, but when in rut, they can become more determined than any other time. Note to new goat owners: This is why you should not keep young bucks with their mothers for more than 3-4 months of age. Most goat breeds tend to go into rut during Autumn. Most of a buck's breeding is performed during the months that range from August to January.

- Mounting: You might be surprised to learn that goat kids will begin mounting each other at a very young age of a few days old. Even though this is getting a jump start in establishing dominance within the herd, they are also getting some practice before becoming grownup goats.

Once they begin to age, the mounting games will take on a more sexual tone.

If you have a few bucks on the property, you may have to separate them during their rut periods so they do not harm each other. It is extremely important to note that you should never turn your back on a buck during a rut because they can be aggressive with humans.

Are Goats Intelligent?

Have you ever stared at a goat and wondered what they were thinking, and how smart they might be? Well, wonder no more because goats have a pretty impressive IQ! According to researchers for both the Queen Mary University of London and the Institute of Agricultural Science in Switzerland (2014), they found that goats might be more intelligent than they seem. During their studies, they learned that they dwell in complex social groups and are expert climbers. Because they live a considerable length of life, they believe that goats are able to build up a library of memories and skills more easily than other short-lived animals. Goats are adept at attaining hard-to-reach foods and despite the rumor that they eat garbage (although they do eat or nibble on things that surprise us), they can be picky eaters.

Researchers from the Queen Mary University of London went on to challenge 12 domesticated goats, believing that because of their domestication, they now lacked the ability to forage as well as their wild cousins. In a test designed to find out if goats had intelligence, researchers borrowed a page from primate scientists and placed some fruit inside of a box, which could only be accessed by the goats solving a puzzle. In order to solve this task, the goat would have to use their teeth to pull on a rope, thereby activating a lever. They would then have to use their muzzle to move the lever up, releasing their fruit reward for them to enjoy. Their end results showed that 9 of the 12 were able to master the task after around four attempts. The three goats that failed tried to circumvent the test by using their horns to pry open the box.

To test their long-term memory, researchers waited 10 months and presented the 9 goats that passed initially with the same food box puzzle to determine how long it would take them to repeat their success and obtain their snack. Every one of the 9 remembered how to receive their fruit and did so in less than a minute, showing long-term memory.

Be Prepared

Whenever you choose to add any animal to your life, you should always take its lifespan into account. No animal should be added to your life due to an impulse, and a goat is no exception. Goats breeds may differ on the length of life expectancy and of course, there will always be those exceptions that live far beyond a normal lifespan for that breed.

Generally, a doe can be expected to live 11 to 12 years when in good health. If you choose to breed your goat after the age of 10 it is likely to have a pregnancy-related death as opposed to does that retire from the breeding program early, thus enjoying a longer life expectancy. Due to the stresses centered around rut, it is unusual for bucks to live past the age of 10, while wethers (a castrated male goat), can live longer than bucks, usually between 11 and 16 years.

Below you will find lifespans broken down by breed and some of the more popular breeds—these may surprise you!

- Alpine goats live 8-12 years and are hardy and weather tolerant.
- Angora goats live over 10 years (generally into their teens) if they have received good care.
- Boer goat bucks have a lifespan of 8-12 years, while the does can live 12 - 20 years! This particular breed can attribute their long life to a natural resistance to disease.
- Kiko goats are a large meat breed of goat and have shown that they are disease and parasite-resistant. This breed often lives 8-12 years.
- LaManche goats are a dairy breed and have a shorter life expectancy than many other breeds. They live between 7-10 years.
- Myotonic goats (also known as *fainting* goats) can live up to 15 years and are quite hardy.
- Nigerian Dwarf goats are usually the go-to goat for smaller dairy farms. They have excellent quality milk and this makes them a frequent favorite by most owners. They live around 15 years.
- Nubian goats are used for milk, meat, and hides. While they don't produce a large volume of milk, it is higher in butterfat than most and more flavorful, making excellent cheese. One drawback is that they are very vocal, so get ready for 15-18 years of noise!
- Oberhasli goats are smaller goats with gentle and calm dispositions. They live 8-12 years.

- Pygmy goats are popular for smaller operations. This small and friendly breed is one of the most commonly kept for pets, but can be used for meat and milk production. They live for about 12 years.
- Pygora goats are primarily a fiber breed and were created by breeding white angora goats to purebred pygmy goats. If taken good care of, you can expect them to live 12-15 years.
- Saanen goats can live past 15 years and are associated with heavy milk production.
- Toggenburg goats live 8-12 years and are characterized as being friendly and curious. They will most often fit the role of pet or dairy goat.

By and large, goats are mostly sweet animals that grace your farm and clear your land, in addition, they can help you produce some excellent products. When there is nothing on television, just pull up a chair and watch your goat buddies entertain you.

Types and Breeds of Goats

What goat breeds you choose will depend upon your interest.

Dairy Goats

- Alpine goats originated in France and when they arrived in 1922, there were only twenty-one animals imported to the United States. They are hardy animals that thrive in virtually any climate.

- Guernsey dairy goats were developed from the rare Golden Guernsey goats. The Golden Guernsey is an English breed that is highly desirable by American goat lovers. The importation of this animal is currently impossible, but Guernsey-type animals are being bred by crossing Swiss dairy goats with Golden Guernsey semen. It is thought that these golden-haired dairy goats likely originated in Greece and Syria. This breed of goat is also considered rare (see below).

- LaMancha goats most likely originated from the Murciana, which was on exhibition at the 1904 Paris World's Fair. They arrived in California with Spanish missionaries, and by the 1920s, the descendants of the LaMancha had been crossed with Toggenburg bucks. They are known for their pixie-like ears and gentle, curious personality.

- The Nigerian Dwarf was originally introduced in the United States from West Africa by zoos to feed their large cats, but their gentle nature soon brought these minis to popularity as a pet. At one time, their future was at risk, but with their popularity as a dairy goat, they are well on their way to recovery from the Conservation Priority List.

- The Nubian goat was born from a combination of English goats and goats from other parts of the world. During the 1800s, some goats were brought to France from Nubia in North Africa. The Nubian-type goat came to America around 1896, but the first traceable animals were registered around 1918.

- Oberhasli goats at some point in the early 1930s were imported into the United States from the Oberhasli region of Switzerland. This breed was originally known as the Swiss Alpine, but in 1979, the American Dairy Goat Association (ADGA) recognized the Oberhasli as a separate breed. This breed was also listed on the endangered list, but is now growing in popularity and increasing in numbers.

- Saanen goats received their name from the Saanen Valley in the southern area of Switzerland. Between the years of 1904 and

1930, there were about 150 Saanens imported to the United States.

- The Sable goat was a late bloomer and only recognized as a separate breed by the ADGA in 2005. This breed was brought about by a recessive gene within the bloodlines of the Saanen goat, making the Sable a colored Saanen.
- The Toggenburg was among the first purebred dairy goats to come to the United States. The breed originated from the Toggenburg Valley of Switzerland.

Fiber Goats

- Angora goats journeyed to the United States in 1849.
- Cashmere goats are sheared once each year and can yield as much as 2.5 pounds of *fleece*. A cross between an Angora and Cashmere goat is called a Cashgora.
- Until fairly recently, Angora goats were only bred to be white, but recently, there has been some interesting breeding practices going on that has resulted in a Colored Angora goat.
- Nigora goats are created by crossing a smaller breed with their larger counterpart breed. Therefore, this cross between an Angora and a Nigerian Dwarf resulted in the Nigora. The

breed association for this animal was formed in 2007.

- Pygoras are the result of another small-breed cross. Angora does were bred to Pygmy bucks in order to become a favorite with hobbyist breeders and pet owners. The Pygora Breeders Association was formed in 1987.

Meat Goats

- Boer goats were originally developed in South Africa and came to the United States by way of New Zealand because the USDA restricted the direct import of goats directly from Africa. By the year 1995, however, these restrictions were lifted, and the embryos were permitted to be sent directly from South Africa.
- The Kiko was bred in New Zealand by a group crossing Anglo-Nubian, Toggenburg, and Saanen bucks. Four generations later, a new breed of meat goat was created.
- Myotonic goats are also known as the fainting goat. This goat breed has a unique condition called myotonia congenita. What this means is that when the animal is startled, their muscle cells tighten and this can result in a momentary stiffening of the legs which causes them to *faint*.

- The Savanna goat was also a breed that was developed in South Africa around the year 1957.
- Spanish Meat goats have ancestral ties back to the sixteenth century and traveled with Spanish missionaries to the Caribbean Islands. For three hundred years this was the sole goat in the regions of the United States and Mexico.

Miniature Goats

- Pygmy Dwarf goats arrived in the United States from Sweden in 1959. The Pygmy comes in many coat colors and is popular for its playful mannerisms. Pygmies often display bowed legs and display a body that is disproportionate to the size of their legs.
- Mini Dairy goats are miniature versions of the larger dairy breed, but they require less space and feed, making them attractive alternatives to hobby farmers.

Rare Breeds

- Olde English Milche goats were initially brought to the South Pacific in the late eighteenth century. These goats are now extinct in England, but a feral group of goats has thrived in New Zealand for 150 years. According to the Arapawa Registry, there are only 175 of these animals present in the United States.
- San Clemente is a rare breed of goat that inhabits San Clemente Island. There are only about 500 of these animals in existence today.

So, Where Does One Buy Their Goats?

If you have never raised livestock before, you might be scratching your head wondering where you purchase livestock. Let's just assume that you have done all your research and know exactly what breed of goat you want to get started with. You have made some appointments to go look at some goats, but you want to make sure that you don't impulse buy just because they have some really cute goats in the front pasture.

Hopefully, you haven't been lured into a farm with a sign out front that simply states *goats for sale*. You should begin by looking for a potential breeder and make an appointment to go look at their operation and their animals. By checking out their farm, you will know what to look for by following some of my tips:

- Word of mouth. Don't be shy, ask around about the breeder's reputation. If you have a local feed store, strike up a conversation and ask what they think. Chances are excellent that they have a working relationship with the farm by delivering supplies. Local goat owners may have some input about the breeder in question too, and you might inquire if they have bought from this breeder if their animals were healthy and sound.

- Ask to see the entire breeding operation and take a tour, noting the cleanliness of their facility and if there appear to be only healthy animals on the property. Ask to see their breeding stock and any records that they might be able to share with you. Their records should show how well their sale animals perform, and they may even give you some references of buyers regarding their stock. Make notes on how their stock is managed and don't forget to shop around before buying.

- Avoid sale barns. Many times these animals are there for a reason and are being culled. What that means is perhaps that particular line has proven to be a poor dairy producer, they may have bad genetic physicalities, such as a genetically poor topline, poor udder attachment, weak pasterns, or perhaps they are just older animals who are no longer viable to use for breeding stock or have stopped producing dairy altogether.

- Join social media groups, especially if there is a local one that might be able to fill you in on the local breeders.
- Contact your local extension office to see if they might be willing to give you a referral.
- If possible, connect with a local livestock mentor and see if they would be able to share their insight. In my experience, most owners love to talk about their animals.
- Connect with veterinarians in your area that specialize in your intended livestock choice and pick their brain about red flags you should be looking for. (*Note: they will not talk directly about any customers, so keep to generic questions.*)
- Always ask questions.
  - Why are you selling these goats?
  - How old are they?
  - Has this goat ever been bred before, and what were the results?
  - Is the goat registered?
  - Is there any history of disease within this bloodline? Or with just this particular goat?
  - Is your herd CAE-free? (Caprine Arthritis Encephalitis) Any breeder

should be able to provide documentation of this when requested. This is a viral disease spread by the bodily fluids of an infected animal and is much like HIV. The reusing of a needle can spread this disease, as well as spilled milk on the ground. CAE can cause severe arthritis in multiple joints, mastitis, and pneumonia.

○ Is your herd CL-free? (Caseous Lymphadenitis) This is a contagious bacteria-like disease that infects both sheep and goats. The organism itself can enter a goat through an open wound or mucous membranes. It will cause abscesses of the lymph nodes and will most likely display a thick yellow or perhaps green discharge that resembles toothpaste. These abscesses are not limited to just the lymph nodes and can also occur in a goat's organs, such as the liver, udder, or lungs. Once a goat has contracted CL, they will continue to battle with repeat abscess for the remainder of its life. The organisms that create the abscesses, when ruptured, will contaminate the environment and are very difficult to kill. Because of this, they may infect your goats for years. Should your animal experience internal abscesses, they may show signs of chronic weight loss, exercise intolerance, a chronic cough, difficulty breathing, or even sudden death. Once an environment has become contaminated with CL, everything should be burned. In theory, this can be transmitted to humans.

○ Is your herd free from Johne's disease? Also known as paratuberculosis, is caused by an organism found in manure-contaminated environments. Even though kids can become infected from a dam through their milk or even in utero, clinical signs may not appear until the animal is 2-4 years of age. Infected animals will show progressive signs of weight loss even though they eat well and, in addition, the affected goats will appear weak, anemic, have a poor coat, and poor skin quality. It emulates chronic wasting disease that you see in deer species.

● When dealing with a breeder, you should always have papers in hand before you leave with your livestock. Registration papers should never be *mailed*.

Your goat business is an investment and should always be treated like a professional business transaction.

Reputable breeders will never have any problems producing the necessary paperwork you will need to register your goat, nor will they be offended by any questions you might have.

Reasons to Buy a Registered Goat

1. If you want to be able to breed as part of your operation, you will be able to connect with more people that own registered goats. Even customers that are just starting their first herd, will typically want to buy a registered animal. Without a registered herd, you will risk reducing your customer base.
2. Registered goats will have generations to back up their bloodline, enabling potential owners to track their lineage.
3. Registered goats will have the ability to be entered in shows and contests, for example, county fairs and 4-H competitions.
4. Your registered goats will always be able to command a higher price than an unregistered equal.

Questions to Ask a Breeder Before Purchasing Your Goat

1. THE most important question (see above for why) to ask of your breeder is if their herd has

been tested for CAE, CL, and Johnes. They should be able to supply you with all results.

2. You should ask for pictures of the goats being purchased from all angles.

3. Confirm that all the registered paperwork will be included at the time your sale is finalized. You can always request that they email you a copy or take a picture and include it in a text message.

4. Ask them what goat organizations they belong to and which one their herd is registered with.

5. Always ask them about their feeding practices, health practices, worming, and any general maintenance they follow with their herd.

Reasons to Look for Another Breeder

If you are feeling uncomfortable about a deal, or you are feeling pressured by the breeder, you always have the option of walking away and calling it a day. Learn to listen to your intuition.

1. Lack of important testing papers for CAE, CL, and Johnes

2. No photos

3. Lack of or insufficient paperwork

4. An inability to list what is included in your purchase

5. Poor information regarding the goat's Dam and Sire

6. Do you notice that the living conditions for the prospective goats and their herd seem unhealthy?

Do You Have Reservations?

Do you have reservations about getting into goat ownership? If you are a novice, goats can seem extremely less intimidating than jumping headfirst into cows just by size alone, but many people get into goats without thinking everything through. While it's true that goats are less expensive than cows, there are some things to consider before making that final commitment. You should be aware of every aspect of ownership before you dive right in. Make sure that you are committed!

1. Were you aware that goats need their hooves trimmed on a regular basis and that this can also play a part in their overall health? Overgrown hooves can make it hard for your goats to get around and could end up causing them arthritis and lameness issues. If you are planning on performing this yourself, you may need to look into the best methods out there.

2. Fencing challenges can arise because every goat is a reincarnation of Harry Houdini. If you think that your fence line is perfect, think again. Goats will always be able to escape, and it can

happen on a daily basis. Even providing them with an enticing playground and ample pasture will still not always be enough to keep them on the correct side of the fence.

3. Deworming. One thing that goats are prone to get is intestinal worms, and you will need to stay on top of their overall health by practicing deworming regularly using herbal or chemical options. By the same token, you must be careful not to over deworm your goats because worms are becoming more resistant to all of our market chemicals.

4. If you want to have goat milk, you have to have a buck. Without breeding your does, you will not get milk, but the downside is that you have to deal with a buck. Your buck, to put it mildly, will smell. If I put it honestly, they will stink to high heaven, but only during their *rut*. It seems that the true ladies' man will stink bad enough to make you vomit because they rejoice in playing in their own pee and that of others.

5. Say goodbye to your landscaping and vegetable garden once you have goats. Not only will you have to remove any toxic plants that might injure or kill your goats, but everything else will be eaten down to the ground. If the promise of homemade soft goat cheese outweighs your green thumb, then you may be alright embracing their quirky behavior.

6. Castration. If you are a beginner, you will probably need many more miles under your belt before you are ready to contemplate performing this action. If you are unsure or just plain don't want to deal with castration, you can always lean on your veterinarian.

Any young bucks that are not considered as replacement bucks for your future breeding program should be castrated between the ages of 2 to 4 weeks. Young bucks are fully capable of breeding does as early as 4 to 5 months of age. There are three common ways to castrate your bucks, and we have listed these below:

1. An elastrator is an inexpensive and quick method of castration that is a bloodless method. You would put a heavy rubber ring around the scrotum near the goat's body. This ring will block any blood circulation reaching the scrotum and testicles, causing them to dry and shrivel, sloughing off in 10 to 14 days. This method can only be done when the scrotum is small (from three days to three weeks of age, depending upon your breed's size). This method will rely on the fact that the scrotal muscles and tissues are still underdeveloped.

Your first step is to put the rubber ring on the prongs of the elastrator and while the male kid is restrained, you will pass the scrotum through the open ring, and you should see the prongs of the elastrator facing the kid's body. You must be able to feel the scrotum and make sure that both testicles are in the scrotum below the ring. The rubber ring that is positioned close to the goat's body should then be slipped off the elastrator prongs. When performing this, you must not inadvertently injure the rudimentary teats of the male kid.

There should be minimal discomfort to your animal until the area becomes numb, however, you should always monitor your kids during the period prior to the sloughing off step. This method does run a higher risk of tetanus than other castration methods. Should the banded scrotum not fall off within an appropriate amount of time, then it will need to be removed manually.

2. Burdizzo® is another quick and bloodless method of castration using a Burdizzo clamp that will emasculate, or crush and rupture the spermatic cords. While this method can be used on older animals, if you follow my advice, you

will castrate your animals when they are young.

The spermatic cords must be crushed one side at a time, and you should have your animal restrained during this process. Grabbing the scrotum, you will need to manipulate one of the testicles deep within the scrotal sac and locate the spermatic cord. You will then place the clamp over the spermatic cord one-third of the way down the scrotum. After you have performed this, clamp down and hold for 15 to 20 seconds. Afterward, release the clamp and reposition it over the spermatic cord one-half inch lower and repeat the procedure. You will then mirror these steps on the other side to crush the other spermatic cord. ALWAYS check the position of the spermatic cord before and after each clamping to make sure that no mistakes are made. When using this method, the scrotal sac will not slough off but will remain on your animal. The testicles on your kid will atrophy and disappear.

During fly season, this method works well because there are no open wounds. The goats should be between four weeks and four months of age, with an ideal window of 8 to 12 weeks being optimal. It can be difficult to tell sometimes if the spermatic cords have indeed been crushed. Therefore, this method may be less reliable than other methods.

3. A knife is the third method of castration and often results in less stress for the animal. Ideally, the animal should be restrained and the scrotal area washed. The hands of the person performing the task should be washed and sanitized with alcohol. The scrotum is then gripped, and the testicles should be pushed to the upper portion and the lower third of the scrotum is then cut off. The removal of the lower third allows for wound drainage and helps fight against infection. Each testicle is slowly pulled down and away from the kid's body until the cord breaks. If your subject is more than 4 to 5 weeks old, you should take the knife and scrape through the cord rather than wait for it to break (this creates less bleeding). The remaining part of the scrotum is then sprayed with an antibacterial spray that will repel or kill flies. It will not be unusual for your kids to be lethargic for a few days, but they will recover and be their normal bounding selves. Following common sense, your kids should not be

in an area that is muddy or filthy while they recover from this procedure.

Housing Needs

Every animal needs shelter and there are always going to be general shelter tips that will work almost anywhere, but sometimes regional ideas will apply, so we would recommend to always study what people who live around you do. For example, if you live in Texas, you probably wouldn't build the same kind of building needed for severe winter weather in another part of the country. Ideally, if you have a large herd, you may want to practice pasture rotation in order to rest a field, but you would still need shelters that could move easily without tearing up your fields. Of course, if money is no object, you can build two separate permanent shelters and just move your goats.

There is no one correct way to build a shelter, but they should provide protection from drafts and elements like rain, sun, or heavy winds. Running water makes it easier to refill buckets, water troughs, or perhaps you want to splurge and install an automatic waterer.

Having electricity is beneficial when it starts getting dark early or if you want to power water heaters for winter, run some clippers, or add a needed heat lamp for your newborn kids.

If you live in a northern climate, you will need a shelter that can protect your herd from snow, ice, and the eventual flooding when wintry precipitation finally melts. Having your shelter face the south will provide the best protection against winds.

Believe it or not, the breed you choose to raise can also make a difference in what kind of shelter you invest in. Dairy goats tend to have a lower body score condition (more on that later) than a meat goat breed because they use up most of their body's energy-making milk instead of staying warm.

While there are some ingenious inventions out there to improve your goats' comfort, we recommend touring some local goat shelters to help you make up your mind on what to build. One thing that is important no matter where you live is ventilation. Without proper airflow, you can run the risk of an ammonia build-up, which can cause respiratory issues within your herd.

According to Jodi Helmer (2020), you should avoid building materials such as plywood, plastic, or areas with unprotected insulation. The floors should be made of dirt, concrete, sand, or gravel. We do not recommend wood flooring as this will soak up urine, and besides being impossible to clean, will hold in the ammonia smell.

Shelters are usually located on the highest point of your property, so rain and melting snow will drain away from the building. Keep in mind whether you are utilizing a shelter or barn, it should be accessible for the delivery of supplies. For this reason, many hobby farmers opt to keep the shelter and their herd closer to their homes for convenience.

Starting with a smaller shelter is easier for new owners so they can get some experience with running their small operation before making decisions on a grander scale. Starting smaller with a preexisting barn or shed of some kind will give you a chance to construct more permanent housing.

Avoid Overcrowding

Just because you are starting small, you still need to offer your animals space. To avoid overcrowding, your basic shelters should have a rear eave height of 4 - 6 feet and the front eave should stand around 6 - 8 feet. You should figure that each goat requires between 8 - 10 square feet of floor space as a minimum. A better standard for measurement would be 12 - 25 square feet per animal (especially if you have larger goats instead of the dwarfs or minis). So, if you have, for example, a herd of 10 goats, your starter shelter would measure between 120 - 250 square feet.

Again, ranges in shelter size can be greatly affected by the climate that you live in. If your herd is found in a place where you have a considerable amount of winter weather or rainy weather, your goats will be spending more time inside versus a dryer climate. Should you have a large pasture and a milder climate, your goats will likely spend more time outside on their playground equipment than inside the barn.

Animal Welfare can also dictate how much space you must provide. Animal Welfare Approved (2020) rules dictate that any dairy goat weighing no more than 44 pounds must have a minimum of 4 square feet of space per animal. If you provide less than adequate space, the less dominant or smaller herd members may be pushed out into the elements if there is a shortage of space.

Overcrowding can also play a part in health issues, like mite outbreaks. With the goats all snuggled up in smaller areas, it can cause the spread of various health concerns, and it will also be more difficult to keep clean.

You should take the size of your goats into consideration and build a tall enough roof accordingly. Should you build too short of a shelter, your goats might decide to jump on the roof, which will cause damage not only to your shelter but also to members of your herd. Another problem that you may not consider when building a lower roof is that a human needs to be able to fit underneath in order to effectively clean the shelter.

Speaking of clean shelters, it is essential to your herd's health to remove any manure and soiled bedding. You should plan on cleaning and disinfecting your shelter regularly.

Adding Kids?

The best-laid plans are often tossed out the window when you suddenly find out that you have kids on the way! Even if you don't plan on keeping any offspring, you still need to provide certain amenities for their health and well-being.

Pregnant does and newborns come with their own specific shelter needs. They will need a secluded pen that provides them with extra protection from the elements and a safe outlet that can be used for a heat lamp.

Kids can be extremely fragile and if not provided with adequate shelter requirements, they can succumb to respiratory infections and hypothermia due to cold, wet weather. In extreme cases, the elements can even cause their death.

Does and kids should be separated from the herd for a minimum of 3 - 5 days after birth. This private space not only provides them with adequate shelter needs but will allow you to assist with deliveries should that be necessary, and the private area also gives the does and kids time to bond without interference from the rest of the herd.

Adding the Essentials

Ideally, your shelter will be more than a house for your herd; it should also be a storage building for your hay, grain, minerals, equipment, and any other supplies. Goats will always need access to their feeders, free-choice minerals, and of course, water, but you may want to incorporate a milking station into your design, or a designated area in which you will attend to their hoof trimmings or shearing.

While many people share housing between goats and other livestock, it is always best to provide a separate shelter for your goats. Chickens can add additional mess to goat quarters and if your hay is not covered properly or up high enough, the chickens can poop on the hay, causing sanitation issues and health problems. We have even heard stories of finding a dead chicken in a goat area. What happened we will never know, perhaps they trampled her or head-butted her, but the result was a sad one.

Sheep and goats can get along, but each species exhibits different behavior from the other. Both of these species can share the same diseases and parasites, so it may be more beneficial to keep them separated. Also, when feeding, sheep will not tolerate copper, which may be found in your goat feed and minerals. Since they are different animals with different mannerisms, they will probably not be happy together. If you are fortunate, they will merely ignore each other. Sheep, like goats, are herd animals and will need another of their species. There have been people I have known that say that their goats were just pesky bullies and acted aggressively toward their sheep.

How to Survive the Winter

If you happen to live in an area where you are subject to severe winter weather, then there are some other plans you will need to make. All of your livestock will find winter more stressful than other times of the year, but being a great owner, you will be able to give supportive care by adjusting your care, feeding, and overall management of your herd.

The most important winter adjustment to make to protect your goats is to block any cold north winter winds and keep them warm and dry. If you have been following good nutritional practices for your animals, then they will have grown a thick coat of hair to help them survive the winter chill. In addition, you will have to provide plenty of clean, dry bedding, and if you have goats kidding in the cold weather, they will require extra shelter because the young goats will not be able to maintain their body temperature. Most in these situations will require a heat lamp, but these will need to be monitored with caution because of the added risk of barn fires or if your animals can reach and chew on electrical cords. Your herd will grow furry coats to help keep them insulated through the winter, and most breeds will have a two-layer coat consisting of longer hairs on top and a fluffy cashmere layer underneath. It is important to provide your herd with mineral supplements that support healthy fur growth, like copper and zinc.

It might seem like a large investment, but insulation is key for areas that experience winter months. Keeping your animals safe, warm, and comfortable will make it all worth it.

Along with insulation, you want good ventilation while keeping drafts at bay. Cold air can accumulate at the floor level of your barn and can create toxic gases, but with proper ventilation, those unhealthy aspects will be pushed out, bringing warm clean air from the barn ceiling downward. Improper ventilation will cause cold air to blow on your goats, and those drafts can make your herd susceptible to illnesses, such as pneumonia.

Fresh clean water is a constant need for all livestock and if you do not have some sort of heating source, you will need to change their water several times each day to remove ice. Any sort of heating device will need to be monitored for chewing. Should you be fortunate enough to have a heated automatic waterer, those cords will be encased in the unit and the only thing you will need to do is freshen the water when it becomes dirty.

Your goats will require more roughage to help them maintain their body temperature during cold winter months. You may need to add feedings of alfalfa or mixed hay. Alfalfa hay, in particular, is a great source of both energy and protein for your livestock. However, when feeding bucks and wethers, the extra protein can cause urinary calculi. This disease can affect both goats and sheep and will prevent urination and breeding; this illness can and does have the ability to kill your animals.

Unless you have splurged on radiant heat (and yes, there are some that have!), you should provide your goats with a resting or sleeping place that is up off the ground on platforms. Fresh deep bedding and platforms will give your goats somewhere to lie down on a surface that isn't cold, dirt, or concrete, which can pull heat from their bodies.

Even if there is snow on the ground, but the sun is shining, make sure that your goats go outside and move about and play, even if it's only for a few hours. Activity helps them create heat and remedies the boredom that they may experience when it is bitterly cold and conditions prevent them from going outside. Providing multiple feeding stations is a good way to get your goats moving around and jockeying for position.

Eew, Lice!

Goat lice tend to be more prevalent during the winter months and these strains of lice are host-specific, meaning that they only attack goats and species that are similar, such as sheep. The lice strains that will plague your goats are divided into two groups: the Anoplura (sucking lice) and the Mallophaga (chewing or biting lice).

You can recognize the signs of lice by your animal's dull coat and excessive rubbing, itching, scratching, and biting behavior. If your goat is suffering from sucking lice, you may also see scabby, bleeding areas that can quickly turn into bacterial infections if not treated quickly.

It is recommended that you work together with your veterinarian to plan ahead for any treatments needed to keep a lice outbreak under control. They will recommend either topical or systemic treatments depending upon which kind of lice you are addressing. Biting lice can be controlled with a liquid or powder applied topically and while sucking lice can be treated in the same fashion, it usually requires a systemic treatment (oral or injectable). Since there is no treatment currently labelled for or approved for goats, you must treat under the advice of your veterinarian. Remember to follow your vets directions exactly as there may be specific waiting times for milk or meat harvests.

If you suspect that your animals have lice, one of the best places to look for the parasite is just behind the foreleg on the skin. The lice may look like dirt between the hair and the skin. You have to wait and watch for movement to properly identify it. You may also see some eggs attached to your goat's hair follicles.

Telltale signs of goats that might be infected include dull coats, exhibit excessive biting, scratching, rubbing, and grooming behavior. You may even notice patches of missing or thinning hair. If you are raising goats for fiber, this can greatly affect the value of their harvest due to low hair quality. Bites from the Anoplura can develop into bacterial infections, but the greatest threat to your herd because of lice is anemia, which can cost them their lives.

The presence of lice can add stress to your animals because they will feel anxiety and discomfort. As a result, they may even go off their feed, causing weight loss and an increased inability to stay warm in the cold months. If you have dairy goats, they will likely experience a drop in milk production up to 25 percent.

Don't feel like you have let your animals down because any herdsman can have infected animals; cold climates and being confined are unfortunately ideal conditions for a lice infestation. Certainly, don't let this discourage you about your care because lice are typically seasonal and show the highest amount of activity during the late winter to early spring. When extended sunshine and warmer temperatures return, lice tend to disappear, but don't believe that you can put off treatment because the health issues will not leave with the lice.

Don't Fence Me In

Oh, give me land, lots of land under starry skies above, don't fence me in."

— Cole Porter

What would a habitat for your goats be without an enclosure to keep them and the rest of your property safe? Chaos, that's what! And while your goats might enjoy their freedom, they will not be safe.

Fencing is incredibly important to get right since goats are such escape artists. What you read about their abilities might give you some second thoughts about bringing them home, but here are some tips I have gathered to make your fencing efforts more solid:

1. All design aspects of your fencing should target keeping your goats inside the area. We all like nice-looking things, but when it comes to fencing, functionality is of the utmost importance. What we are hinting at here is that you might have to let the idea of adorable fencing be saved for another day and for another purpose. The fact is that if a goat really wants to get out, it probably will. What you ultimately decide to use should at least put up a good fight.

    Wooden posts placed in the ground are best supported by concrete overshoes. After that, livestock fencing is a good choice and smaller mesh typically is a better choice than the larger mesh. The smaller the holes, the harder time they will have passing through it. To be honest, no matter how well you plan, if they really want to get out, they will find a way.

2. Besides keeping your goats in, it should also keep predators out. Even if your area seems devoid of predators, it is in your best interest to plan like you have an abundance of potential predators. With that in mind, your fence should be sturdy and tall. Frankly, the best defense against coyotes is to put a donkey out in the pasture with your goats because, even at 6 feet tall, coyotes can still find a way to jump in and get to your goats.

   Donkeys will attack a predator and can be extremely aggressive while using both their teeth and hooves to confront an attacker. Often your sheep or goats will perceive the donkey as their protector and will gather nearby if they think there is a threat. Should you choose to add a donkey or two and integrate them with your herd, you should keep in mind that the shelter will need to be taller to accommodate the bigger animal. If you add a donkey to your herd, be aware that they should never have access to Rumensin, or any other feeds or supplements intended for your ruminants.

3. Electric fencing can be a good option, especially if you are located near a rather busy road. It is a

small inconvenience to shock your goats until they get used to it and figure out they should stay away from it. Depending on how large of an area you need to electrify, it can be a bit expensive, but if you live close to a busy road, it might be worth it, so you don't worry so much about your goats getting loose and getting hurt or causing an accident.

While you may experience some initial internal struggles about shocking your animals, it is not that strong of a current, and if it keeps them from being harmed or killed, it is worth the expense.

If you are relying on electric fencing alone, the recommended number of strands is seven. Your best option is to use a single strand with a mesh fence. Apparently, there is a new electric fence on the market that features woven wire that you may want to look into.

4. Your fence must be strong. Especially if you have male goats, you should consider the smaller mesh livestock fencing or even invest in more expensive livestock panels.

5. Maintaining your fencing is imperative. Regular fence maintenance should be made part of your routine. Walking the fence line will help you notice any holes or other areas that need your immediate attention and mending. When you

do this, you should always check the gates and latches to ensure that nothing needs repair. If you have installed electric fencing, you should periodically use a fence tester to make sure that the current is still working properly.

6. Keep your goats happy on their side of the fence! If they love their play areas, their bed, and their feeding schedule, then they are far less likely to roam. If you find that your goats are trying to escape a lot, you may want to change things up in their pasture.

Woven wire and chain link can also be good options for your fence. The heavy gauge of a chain link can last for some time, but it must be heavily secured.

Goats Love to Climb

Get ready to watch endless rounds of king of the mountain between your goats. They love to climb on anything and everything (including cars). Your goats will probably perform some impressive things, and some goats can even climb trees.

Over the years, goats have evolved to perform tough climbs and daring jumps and this is primarily because they possess two toes on each of their hooves, which has given them an advanced sense of balance for scaling things that amaze and astound us. There's a good chance that when you see a photo of a goat standing in a tree, it has not been photoshopped.

Planning Ahead

Advance preparation is key when you are bringing home your first herd. It can be a very exciting time for you, but the last thing you want to happen is to discover that you forgot an important supply for your new herd and the local farm store is closed. We suggest that you make some checklists regarding your new shelter and supplies to make sure that you have everything that you need.

- Shelter
    - Secure fencing should be in place. Netting and wire will both work, but the key is to make sure that it will (ahem) keep your goats in and possible predators out. Electric fencing may create some added protection.
    - Hay mangers, because once a goat drops hay on the floor, it will not eat it.
    - Hay
    - Water buckets, small water trough, or automatic waterer
    - Salt
    - Free choice minerals for goats (always choose *chelated minerals*)

- Free choice baking soda, which should always be offered to prevent indigestion or bloat in your herd.
- Kelp is an option for your pregnant or lactating does. Always pick *chelated mineral-free* varieties.
- Medical Kit (a more detailed list is found in chapter 6)
  - Digital thermometer
  - Pepto Bismol
  - Electrolytes for dehydration (can use Gatorade)
  - Probios probiotics for gut health, especially after an illness
  - Drench syringe for the administration of oral meds
  - Aerosol antiseptic bandage protector (Blu-Kote, AluShield)
  - Dewormer
  - Bandages
  - Gauze
  - Medical tape
  - Alcohol swabs
  - Iodine
  - Hydrogen peroxide
  - Healing salve like Neosporin
  - High-potency B complex in case of goat polio
  - 6 cc syringes and needles

- Additional Supplies (many of these focus on kids)
  - Milk replacer
  - A clean bottle, a wine, or soda bottle will do
  - Nipple(s)
  - Grain or alfalfa pellets to offer as a weaning adjusting supplement
  - Vaccinations: CD&T (This is a goat vaccine for use in healthy goats to aid in the prevention of enterotoxemia which is caused by Clostridium perfringens and provides long-term protection against tetanus. USDA approved.
  - Straw bedding

Feeding Your Goat

If you don't know much about goat nutrition, that's okay because that's what we are here for! For the record, goats do not eat tin cans, but they might check out inside to see if there is something yummy leftover. The closest animal that goats resemble for nutritional needs is the deer. Goats are considered ruminants and eat plants, digesting them through a four-compartment stomach system. This is not to be confused with the misinformation that goats have four stomachs. What they have is one stomach with four compartments.

Contrary to popular belief, goats are actually picky eaters. They may taste many things but not eat the entire stalk. There are some goats that harbor suspicions regarding their new foods and might be on the verge of starving before they give in and try out the new taste. Unlike their livestock counterparts, sheep and cattle who tend to eat mostly grass, goats should not eat a diet composed entirely of fresh grass.

Proper attention to feeding will ensure that your herd lives longer, produces more, and has fewer health issues. Any changes in diet should be made slowly so that you might be able to spot any red flags regarding the recent changes. The best practice is to not make any sudden or drastic changes to your herd's diet because this can lead to digestive upset.

Hay

Hay is the main source of a goat's nutrients besides their range, and the hay can be a grassy bale or can include legumes like clover or alfalfa. Always purchase the best quality hay you can locate. Good hay will always be expensive, but the better the hay, the less need you will have for supplementation or added grains. Especially if you are running a dairy barn, good-quality hay will influence the amount and quality of milk you receive from your animals. Hay can be fed freely or just twice a day. The average goat will ingest about 4.5 pounds of hay a day per 100 pounds of body weight. Remember to limit hay to smaller feedings in mangers if you have great pasture since once the hay touches the floor the goats will not eat it.

Tip: If you feed your goats a low-quality forage, all they will do is play with it or pee on it.

Goats require additional hay to boost their roughage intake in order to keep their rumen functioning properly. You should never expect to feed your herd solely on pasture. The rumen is their first stomach compartment and this uses long fiber-like hay to keep the rumen rich in live healthy bacteria. Alfalfa hay or grass alfalfa mix is a popular hay choice for feeding goats and provides them with more protein, vitamins, and minerals than most grass hays. Alfalfa hay will also provide more calcium for feeding your milk-producing goats.

For those of you unfamiliar with a product described as chaffhaye, this is made by using an early cutting of alfalfa or grass and chopping it into fine pieces, and then mixing it with molasses and a probiotic culture for gut health, called bacillus subtilis. After the ingredients are combined, the end product is vacuum-packed. The hay will further ferment while contained, which will add beneficial bacteria that target the goats' ruments. You can feed chaffhaye as an alternative to hay, but realize that this product will be more nutrient-dense than hay. For example, a 50-pound bag of chaffhaye will roughly equal 85 to 100 lbs of hay.

Educate yourself on hay quality found within your region. Hay stored under the roof of a protective barn will retain most of its nutritional value for up to a year. Watch for hay that has been baled and put up still wet or damp because not only is this a fire hazard, but it can lead to mold and microorganisms. These, in turn, will release toxins that can cause your animal to become ill. Never feed your goats moldy hay!

Grain

A good rule of thumb is to have your hay tested for nutrient values because hay is going to differ depending upon where you live and the soil content. It can also differ from year to year due to drought and other environmental issues. Since there is no such thing as perfect hay, this will provide you with what is lacking in your pasture and hay that you can then take the results to an animal nutritionist to devise a plan of attack for your herd's diet. Depending upon the size of your herd, you may want to have a custom feed designed by your livestock nutritionist.

A grain feed or a pelleted mix will add protein, vitamins, and minerals to your goat's diet. Your use of grain will vary, but unless it has been a terrible year for hay production and your pastures are empty, grain products are only a supporting player in your nutritional foundation. There are always exceptions, such as does that are raising multiple kids or a rash of bad weather, but the basis of your herd's nutrition will always be obtained through foraging.

Overall, grain should never be overfed as it can lead to overweight goats and open them up to illnesses. Your grain bag should provide you with a guaranteed analysis and feed rate that gives you guidelines on how much to feed per body weight. Many feeds will include ammonium chloride to promote a healthy urinary tract.

Besides balancing out a hay deficiency, grains are regulated to show animals and growing, breeding, or lactating animals.

There are medicated feeds that are designed to be fed to young goats for the prevention of coccidiosis (see chapter 6). **MEDICATED FEEDS SHOULD NEVER BE FED TO GOATS THAT ARE PRODUCING MILK USED FOR FOOD.** These are usually very palatable to encourage early-weaned kids to eat.

Loose Free Choice Minerals

There are loose minerals formulated for goats that you should always offer free choice to your animals. When possible, always opt for chelated because those are more bioavailable for your animals. Loose minerals are more desirable since the blocks often contain an overabundance of salt and molasses.

Loose Free Choice Baking Soda

Goats can benefit from free choice baking soda, and many goat breeders offer this to their herd. Most herdsmen feed this to their goats to keep their digestive tract in check. There is no need to mix it into their feed because your herd will self-dose when they feel they need it. According to Manna Pro (2020), baking soda can not only aid in digestive issues, but can help prevent bloat when your animal has overeaten or ingested the wrong food. A goat that is offered baking soda on a daily basis can help balance the pH levels found in the rumen, which works similar to how heartburn relief works with us humans. Since goats are typically escape artists, they may be more prone to eat something that causes stomach upset.

The true goat's diet is not just pasture, but a diet that includes shrubs, weeds, and brambles (which is why they make excellent living bush hogs). Since we keep our herds contained in a pasture, our animals will resort to eating grass once all the brambles are cleared away. Should they consume too much grass, it can overpower the bacteria found in their rumen and cause a case of bloat.

Offer baking soda in its own container and replace it when your goats soil the container.

Kitchen and Garden Scraps

Typically, your goats will generally do fine eating kitchen compost, but eggshells can be a problem. If they are used to it, you should be okay, but you should never overdo amounts or frequency. Raisins, corn chips, stale popcorn, or even a slice of bread might make a nice special treat, but we are not an advocate of providing this to your animals with any frequency. A consistent diet keeps a healthy gut, and adding too many extras can upset the animal's digestive tract.

Meeting the Nutritional Needs of the Older Goat

Goats are considered to be of age at around five-years-old and by eight, many exhibit signs of aging. Your older goats may have some special needs because as they age, their teeth will wear down or even fall out. The elder goat may require support in the way of additional grain or some liquid supplements. Your senior goats may need easier access to food and water, and their stiff joints may prevent them from eating or drinking enough to support themselves. If you are unable to separate the younger and older animals, you will have to watch to make sure that the older goats are getting what they need in order to remain healthy.

Feeding Equipment

Nothing fancy is necessary. In fact, many goat keepers make suitable containers from items found at your local farm store or home improvement center. The Internet is full of many such ideas for you to copy. As we have mentioned, you should have some sort of manger that helps your stock access the hay, but not waste it.

You should also invest in metal or plastic containers with tight-fitting lids to keep any grain or minerals in. This will keep pests, like mice, out of your supplies and keep them free from contamination. You may want to consider:

- Feed storage containers
- Food buckets
- Water buckets
- Hay mangers
- Mineral feeders

You Can Build Your Own Manger

There are almost as many designs for building your own mangers as there are stars in the night's sky. It can be as simple as some hog wire nailed into some sturdy two-by-fours or a store-bought manger that hangs over a stall wall or bolted to a wall. It all depends on how handy you are or how comfortable you are around saws.

There are so many designs for mangers inside and outside. Our best recommendation is to surf the web a bit and find one that works for your farm. If you are as handy as one of my good friends (snicker), you will be ordering them from a supply house.

Body Score Conditioning Chart

Score	Condition	Backbone & Ribs	Loin
1	Very lean	Easy to see and feel Can feel under the ribs	No fat
2	Lean	Easy to feel Smooth Need to use a little pressure to feel ribs	Smooth fat

3	Good	Smooth and rounded Even feel to the ribs	Smooth fat
4	Fat	Can feel backbone with firm pressure No points on spine and no ribs felt Indent between ribs felt with pressure	Thick fat
5	Obese	Smooth No individual vertebra felt No separation of ribs felt	Thick fat Lumpy Jiggles

Chapter 2:

It's Going to be Goat-tastic!

Did you know that goats are fantastic at clearing overgrown bits of land? There is no need to rent a bush hog anymore because your goats can take care of that for you, and they are much less labor-intensive.

Goats for Land Management

If you have heard that goats are capable of clearing unwanted vegetation, invasive plants, and overbearing brush, then you have heard correctly. These little dynamos can clear a lot of unwanted vines and weeds, and the best part is they eat all of it, preventing unwanted regrowth. Mowers will cut weeds down and allow seeds to scatter and reestablish said weed in more places, while your grazing goats will eat the weed, seeds, and often the roots.

Goats will go out in the heat of the sunshine and save you many labor-intensive hours using machinery to clear your land. You will not have to invest in extra fuel, spare parts, and repairs if the machinery is yours; rental fees and transportation issues if you are renting equipment. You will also be able to keep your land clear from toxic herbicides that can cause health concerns with the animals, humans, and pollinators that have access to those treated pastures and the goods potentially grown upon them. Your goats will provide a natural solution and will most likely fertilize as they go.

I already mentioned that grass is not a goats' favorite choice for when they get the munchies, and they are unique in the fact that they have special gut enzymes that enable them to digest any number of plants that would prove toxic to other animals.

So, what plants will they clear? They will completely clear overgrown vines and clear any and all weeds, but you should always be aware of anything growing that might transfer to you or your goods, such as poison ivy and poison oak. The fact is that goats love to eat these, but it will transfer to you if you pet them or milk them. Besides overgrowth, you will have to watch them if they begin to destroy something you don't want them eating, such as young apple trees. You will have to devise protection for any plants or trees that you don't want them to clear.

Believe it or not, there are professional goats that are hired to eat excess vegetation. Wouldn't it be great to get paid to just eat all day? There are actual goat landscaping businesses that will drive their herd about in their own trailer, bringing their convenience to you for a price. If you are struggling with growing goats for food, then starting a goat landscaping business might be a good alternative for you, and many companies that provide this service find that they are booked solid from April through November and clear public and private properties.

The goat grazing business will not utilize fossil fuels, even though the goats do emit a greenhouse gas called methane. All you need is a herd of goats and land to keep them on to get started. As with any herd, probably your biggest expense is hoof trimming (if you don't perform this yourself) and veterinarian bills. Depending upon where you are, most cities don't even require a permit to let a herd of goats chow down on an overgrown field.

Truthfully, people hear about goats clearing land, and not only will it be a novelty for them, but they can practice being green, and possibly placate protestors of other less favorable methods. In any case, it can just be fun and entertaining to watch a herd of goats chow down on unwanted overgrowth. A herd can prove to be the perfect group of employees because they love their work. Should they need a bathroom break, they go right where they are eating, which spreads fertilizer.

According to Rachel Manteuffel (2019), a herd of 28 goats can clear an acre of brush in 10 to 12 days. The average charge from a goat landscaping company can cost 2,500 to 3,000 dollars per acre, plus any unseen expenses. The humans from these companies will dig post holes and put up a fence for their herd, but the prep work is anything but glamorous. It can be a hot, sweaty, buggy day and everyone is in high-top rain boots to protect against chiggers and ticks. It is not a huge moneymaker, but it is a business that you can have all to yourself and enjoy the perks of your goofy goats.

Your Goat Herd Will Help You Deliver Amazing Milk and Cheese

Your herd is going to surprise you, when you realize that your friendly and intelligent goats are going to reward you with some outstanding milk. Your animals will be able to thrive on sloping or flat land, and two does will be able to produce enough fresh milk to feed your family all year long. If you add a few more does to your herd, you will even be able to make your own cheese, yogurt, and ice cream. When you walk through your local grocery store and look at all the cow's milk lining the shelves, it may be hard for you to believe that the world's people overall consume goat milk more than cow milk. Since goats tend to appreciate a varied diet composed of what is available in your pasture, you may want to double-check some of the plants growing in your pasture. For example, if they consume some wild onions, it can really alter the flavor of your milk. Roughage from twigs, bark, or leaves is a good source as well as regular pasture, corn, sunflower stalks, and fine stemmed hay filled with alfalfa or clover.

Milking does should receive 2 to 3 pounds (depending upon feeding recommendations) of a commercial feed. If milk production is important, you will want high-quality hay balanced with a dairy grain ration that provides protein, minerals, and vitamins to support quality milk production.

In order to keep your milk flowing, you will need to breed your does once a year. Dairy goats are usually bred in the fall. However, they can have heat cycles from August to January. Their heat cycle lasts three days, and you should put the buck and does together during this time. Once they have been bred, you should again separate the buck from the does. Kidding will occur around 145 to 150 days after the initial breeding.

Interestingly, does will usually have twins or even triplets depending upon the breed. Your doe will begin producing milk after the kids are born and will continue to produce for up to 10 months. You should give each doe a 'dry period' of about two months before she is again bred and delivers new kids, restarting the milk production.

There should be no problem sharing the milk with the kids. After the kids are two weeks old you can confine them overnight and this will allow you to milk the doe in the morning. After you milk, you can return the kids to the doe, so they can nurse. A great way to get the kids used to being handled by humans is to milk the does twice a day and give the kids bottles.

We have found that the milking process is easier if you feed your does grain while you milk them. Milking will be easy to learn, and you should milk out both udders completely at the same time each day. If you choose to milk twice a day, you should separate your milking times by 12 hours. You should keep your milking equipment and area clean and once you have completed milking, you can cool the milk-filled container quickly by setting it into a large pan that you have pre-filled with cold water for the duration of about 15 minutes. If you stir the milk occasionally with a clean utensil, it will help you cool the milk evenly. After your milk has cooled, you can pour it into clean glass containers and immediately refrigerate it. Remember that everything that touches your milk must be sterile. If you plan on hand-milking, you will need the following equipment:

- Milking Stand
- Stainless-steel milking pail
- Stainless-steel strainer and milk filters
- Dish soap or dairy soap
- Bleach or sanitizer
- Acid detergent
- Clean-up brushes
- Strip Cup
- Mastitis indicators
- Paper towels or dairy towels
- Teat dip, such as Fight Bac®

You will find that people who are used to commercial cow's milk will find the taste of goat milk richer and sweeter.

Goat milk is naturally homogenized because the butterfat globules are smaller than that of cow milk, so they will disperse more easily. But unlike cow milk, the cream will not separate on its own, making goat milk products smoother and creamier. If you want to try your hand at butter, you will need to buy or borrow a cream separator. We will have more on milk products in chapter 3.

The Advantage of Meat Goats

Meat goats can be a profitable avenue to follow for a livestock business. However, meat goats are not for everyone. There is no shame in the discovery that meat goats are not your cup of tea.

If you have decided to raise meat goats, you should know upfront that the most difficult thing about them is giving your managed herd proper nutrition. Just like the human saying, you are what you eat.

As we have mentioned before, you should always buy the best hay you can find and afford. Goats have the quickest metabolism of all the ruminants, so proper nutrition is the building block of the best milk, meat, or fiber that you wish to produce. You should never consider feeding a grain-only diet, believing that you will add weight quickly to your animals. Goats can become bloated or develop enterotoxemia from an imbalance of rumen flora due to feeding an improper amount of roughage in your goat's diet.

You will only require a small amount of acreage to test the waters of the goat meat industry.

Meat goats are a staple in many cultures and are extremely popular in Mexican, Greek, African, and Arabic cuisines. It may surprise you to learn that when taking into consideration all the red meat eaten around the world, 70 percent of it comes from goats! I bet you didn't know that! Within the United States, the largest meat goat operations are found further south, where there seems to be more of a demand for the product. Even though the consumption of goat meat is on the rise, the average American has never eaten goat meat.

The production of goat meat tends to increase when there is a trend in ethnic cooking and when people start to analyze the nutritional content of the meat of the goat when compared to that of other livestock.

Changes in food choices are driven by people becoming more conscious of the environment and the health impacts of what we are eating. Educated consumers are learning to look for grass-fed meat raised under humane conditions. Many of these customers will seek out local products from neighborhood farmers.

Goat meat, when roasted, has the same number of calories as chicken, but the meat contains more minerals and less fat. It will contain the same protein content as beef, but provides 10 percent more iron. When goat meat is a product of grass-fed animals, the result is higher omega-3 fatty acids.

Fiber Production

When you raise goats for their hair coat, these breeds are referred to as fiber goats. People always think of sheep or even rabbits when we talk about products of fiber and have no idea that goats are used to produce natural fibers.

Advanced technology may try to duplicate the comfort, strength, and durability of animal fibers, but fiber artisans and educated people know that man-made fibers are no match for those that nature provides us. Natural fibers are amazing when it comes to their ability to insulate you and keep you warm. Natural fiber will absorb perspiration and will wick it away from your skin, discharging it into the air. Another bonus is that all goat fibers are inherently flame-resistant.

Goats that provide us with fibers, such as angora, cashmere, or mohair will grow a new coat every year. The large commercial angora herds are found primarily in the Southwest, and they produce more than one million pounds of mohair each year!

Cashmere goats through selective breeding have finally become viable in the United States, but because only 4 to 6 ounces of this undercoat are produced each year per goat, this drives up the price of cashmere.

If you are looking to dive into ownership of fiber goats, confirmation should always be one of your top considerations. You will need to look for strong legs and feet, as well as a well-formed mammary system for raising kids. Animals should always possess a good set of teeth and a strong jaw for maintaining proper nutrition.

After confirmation, the next consideration is the fleece, and it should cover as much of the animal's body as possible. You should learn as much about fiber goats as possible before taking the step into ownership.

Types of fiber include:

- Cashmere is produced from the Cashmere goat and their fiber is well known for the lightness, warmth, and softness that this fiber creates.

- Mohair - Angora fiber is called *mohair*. Angora goats are the most efficient fiber-producing animal in the world, and there isn't another animal in the world that produces this product. Angora goats are usually sheared twice a year
- Cashgora is a product made from crossing an angora buck and a cashmere doe, and this fiber is favored by many of the world's top fashion designers.
- Kemp is the long, straight, and brittle hollow hair that can show up on the thighs or the backbone of a fiber goat. These fibers break easily and do not take to dye well. The representation of kemp is one criterion for culling a goat from a fiber-producing herd.

When caring for your fiber herd, the majority of these animals will be raised using range-like conditions. This method of husbandry can create challenges for meeting the nutritional needs of your herd. Once they are sheared, these goats can be prone to becoming chilled from cold or damp weather. These animals should never be exposed to sudden temperature drops, increased winds, or humidity. The end result may be the animals falling ill or even dying.

Even the Goat Manure Can be Used

If you want to create the best growing conditions for your plants, then adding goat droppings can be a great choice, since their dry pellets are easy to collect and tend to be less messy than other types of manure. You can even compost it and use it for mulch.

There are several advantages when using goat manure instead of cow, chicken, or horse manure. One of the best benefits that goat manure has is that it doesn't attract insects or burn plants when fresh. It is relatively odorless and has beneficial properties, such as nitrogen, for better fertilizing.

The best time to add goat manure fertilizer to any garden is in the fall, allowing your soil to absorb the nutrients over the winter. As a goat farmer, many people are happy to come and get it out of your way, so it's likely a simple sign offering it for free will find your pile going down quickly.

If you have an extensive garden, you may want to compost your goat manure, and it is neither hard nor messy. A composted product produced in a bin-type structure will be dry and very rich when you mix in some other materials, such as eggshells, straw, grass clippings, leaves, or even kitchen scraps (though most prefer to leave any meat products out of their compost). It's a good practice to keep your compost moist, and you should turn the layers of your pile on occasion to help increase airflow and break down your materials.

Because goat manure is pelletized, their droppings allow more airflow, which aids in how rapidly the compost mixes. The advantages that composted manure brings is:

- Promoting healthier plant growth

- Adding missing nutrients to your soil
- Increased crop production
- The ability to circumvent harmful chemicals

Goats Can Make Great Companions

You may have no aspirations of raising meat or dairy goats, but you will probably discover that many urban households are keeping their goats merely as pets. Goats can display some very charming attributes and because of their good personalities, they can become a good company for other animals, too. Pygmy and Kinder goats are prone to make excellent companions, and even though all sizes of the goat clan can make a good pet, the smaller breeds are the more popular choice.

Like any animal that graces your life, goat owners are finding that their goats bring them stress relief and their barnyard antics are fun to just sit, watch, and relax to. Pet goats are just as messy as their productive counterparts and owners will still face all the basic goat challenges, such as climbing, destructiveness, and being a picky eater. No matter what job your goats perform, they are all fun and social animals that become very attached to their owners.

Most of these pet goats don't have many demands made upon them other than eating, sleeping, playing, and general entertainment. However, some have learned to be therapy animals and will accompany their humans to assisted-living facilities, battered women shelters, schools, and orphanages.

If you are interested in a therapy goat, you can research The Delta Society. This organization registers many different pets, including goats, for therapy work. Any goat in question must pass a test to show that it is a reliable, predictable, and controllable animal that will pursue visiting with strangers. A registered pet with the Delta Society will always display good manners in public places.

Raising a goat as a pet is not as easy as your typical dogs, cats, or even chickens. They can have requirements that you may not be fully aware of, such as the need to roam, hoof trimming, or the fact that you probably will need another of the species. The best way to prepare is to soul search as to why you want to raise goats as pets. You should always look for goats that have been well handled and therefore, well-behaved. Wild or feral acting goats will not be appropriate to shape into pets.

You may not even want a goat for human companionship. Were you aware that many horse racing stables use goats as companions for their higher-strung equine athletes? It's fairly common to find some goats napping in horse stalls, even at Churchill Downs! Owners and trainers agree that goats can have a steady and calming effect on jumpy racehorses.

Regardless of your goat's vocation, they will still need to follow a good diet, receive annual vaccines, and should see their veterinarian regularly. Keep in mind that all baby animals will grow, and a baby goat is no exception! Even the smaller breeds can mature to be about 60 pounds, so be prepared for the adult goat.

The best choice for pet goats are the wethers or castrated males, and you will find that not only are pet goats affectionate and loving, but they will respond to their name, lay their head in your lap (a good reason to remove horns), and they enjoy being massaged and petted. My suggestion is to stick with the castrated males as the best choice for a pet. Since you will need two, we would recommend two castrated bucks.

There are a few tips we would like to give you if considering owning or raising goats as pets:

- Don't buy kids if they are too young. We recommend you wait until they are over 4 to 5 months of age.
- If you want to have castrated bucks, don't perform this when they are still too young. Sometime after 6 months of age would be appropriate.
- Because castrated bucks tend to get urinary calculi, you should feed them only a small amount of grain.
- DO NOT ROUGHHOUSE WITH YOUR GOATS. Playing rough, especially with young kids, can make for some rude behavior when they are older. Too many games of pushing can make your goat aggressive and dangerous when they are older. Always play gently with your baby goats.
- Never allow your baby goats to jump on you. When they become adults, this can become a very dangerous habit.

- Spend quality time bonding with your goats. They enjoy having their muzzle massaged gently and find it calming to have a physical nearness to you. You may even see them roll back their eyes in pleasure.

- Walk around with your goats on occasion. Both parties will find this pleasurable, but make sure that there are no aggressive animals around that might hurt your goats.

- If you plan on taking your goats anywhere in the car, you should get them used to a pet carrier. Always practice safe driving and give them a good experience, so they don't feel apprehension the next time. Slamming on your brakes will tend to alarm your animal. Always get your goat out of the car immediately after arriving at your destination.

- Always communicate with your vet about your goat's health issues. Any noticeable change should be addressed as soon as possible.

- Take good care of your goats and treat them with the love and respect any living creature deserves.

- Have fun with them!

When all is said and done, goats can be a tremendous benefit to you and the upkeep of your land. Even better, is the fact that they can help you profit from having them around. There are so many options. All you need to do is figure out which direction you want to go!

Chapter 3:

Endless Milk and Cheese

Did you know that August is National Goat Cheese Month?

We have already discussed several aspects of milking goats, their nutritional needs, and their milking schedules when balanced with the needs of their kids, but you probably didn't know that your does can experience their first heat when they are seven-months-old!

When Do Does Stop Milk Production?

If you breed her at 12 months of age, your doe will have her first kid around 18 months of age. Your doe will begin to produce milk immediately after giving birth to her first kid. Any milk production will require a birth cycle to get things rolling. Does will continue to produce milk for many years to come, right up until they are 8 to 10 years old; some even up to 14 years of age. There is no specific age that does will stop producing milk, but a good rule of thumb is whenever you stop milking them or allowing them to be bred.

Do All Does Produce Milk?

Theoretically, all goats that can become pregnant will be able to produce milk, but that doesn't mean that they will all be top producers. If you are looking for a meat breed of goat that is also capable of producing milk, they usually only have enough milk to feed their kids and milk production will drop off for meat goats after a few months following the birth of their kids.

Obviously, dairy goats will be the best milk producers for your farm, and they will produce it for longer periods of time, which will allow you to create some amazing things.

As mentioned earlier, balance milking with kids present, but your kids should always have their mother's milk for at least a couple of weeks after their birth. Goat kids can be bottle-fed if needed, but first, they MUST receive their colostrum.

The first milk that goat kids drink from their mother will contain colostrum. The reason this is important is that this first milk will provide them with needed nutrients and antibodies that will aid in their newborn survival. Without this, they will not thrive.

Should you decide to leave the kids on their mother for the duration of their time together, then the mom will begin to wean the kids on her own around the 6 to 8-week range. At around this time, the kids will be proficient at eating solid foods, such as grass, hay, and grain. When they can do this, they can be weaned off their mother's milk entirely.

How Long Will a Doe Produce Milk if They Are Not Bred Again?

You may intend to hold off breeding your goat once their most recent kid has been weaned, and that's okay because a doe will continue to produce milk up to 10 months after the birth of their kid. However, if you cease milking them routinely (daily), you will run the risk of their milk supply either decreasing in yield or drying up completely.

You can always encourage better milk production by keeping your does happy, and that is a fairly simple thing to do.

- Keep them healthy - watch for any signs of mastitis or other viral condition that causes the mammary glands to become inflamed. If you see red, swollen, or otherwise painful udders you should contact your vet immediately
- Feed a high-protein grain, that little bit of extra energy really helps keep their cycle going
- Always provide plenty of high-protein hay
- Provide high quality chelated free choice minerals

Is There a Benefit to Breeding a Doe Who is Already Producing Milk?

Many goat owners who produce dairy find that rebreeding their does help to increase milk yields and keeps their does natural hormones in check. A doe will always produce the most amount of milk right after giving birth and while their baby is growing up. Should your milking does dry up completely, the only way to restart their production is to once again breed them.

How Much Milk Should You Expect?

In nature, there is never an exact number. Some does will produce more and some will produce less. No matter what your yield, you can be facing some large milk quantities if you have a large herd. Below you will find some average yields for the dairy breeds that are based on a single lactation cycle (275-305 days).

Breed	Average Gallon Production
Alpine	272
LaMancha	252
Nubian	218
Oberhasli	257
Saanen	309
Toggenburg	253

How to Milk a Goat

If you are an old hand at owning a dairy herd, you probably already know not only how to milk a goat, but likely you have some of your own innovations to make the process easier. For those of you just starting out, we included information for those just raising their first herd or who are in the process of buying their first herd.

You may feel overwhelmed by the thought of milking your goats, but really, once you get the gist of it, you will find it quite easy. If you recognize going into this venture that you may be a bit uncoordinated with your hands, your first experience may not go as smoothly as you wish. Don't give up! We have all been beginners at one point or another, and you can always get better. One day, you will look back on your experience and laugh. Let's get started:

1. Begin by having some goodies ready for your does. A mixture of alfalfa pellets and a small amount of grain should do the trick, but you can always add other incentives such as alfalfa hay, fresh weeds, or sprouted barley grass. This will keep them distracted and happy.

2. One really good piece of advice is to keep your doe's udder shaved. This can make it much easier to milk and is also easier to keep cleaned off.

3. Always clean up the udder and teats. We prefer to create my own stash of homemade udder wipes (see below) because they circumvent all the online wipes that contain many chemicals. You want to be sure to squeeze the teat so that you can also wipe that opening well.

4. Perform one squirt out of each teat to flush out any blockages or bacteria present.

5. Take time to inspect that first squirt from each teat. What you are looking for is to make sure there is no sign of blood or clumps of milk, which could be an indication of mastitis.

6. You are now ready to begin milking your first goat. The technique you want to use starts with

you taking a hold of the teat as high as you can (which is a couple of inches into the udder).

7. You will use your thumb and forefinger, squeezing the teat hard, so you can trap the milk in the teat.

8. The hard part to grasp is that you need to keep your thumb and forefinger tight, you will bring the rest of your palm and other fingers together. The pressure this causes is what will squirt the milk out to be collected. If you experience a tiny stream or no milk at all, it's probably caused by not keeping your thumb and forefinger pinching hard enough. Milking is not about the tugging, but rather the pinching and the squeezing.

9. You will continue with these last few steps until you have gotten all the milk out that you can.

10. Here's one tip: when you think you have gotten all the milk you can, take a break for a few seconds, then punch into the does udder lightly to help release any other milk that might be trapped there. This movement simulates what a baby kid would do to help get more milk from the mother. Milk out any more product that you can.

11. When your doe is finished being milked, the udder will have a wrinkled and deflated look.

12. Afterward, you should apply some udder balm to the teat and udder to keep them from becoming sore or chapped.

Homemade Udder Wipes

These wipes contain no chemicals, so you always look for the most holistic alternative if you are uncomfortable with harsh chemicals. If you have several species on your property, good news, they can be used on goats, cows, and sheep!

Ingredients

- 1 package (100 wipes) dry disposable wipes
- 2 C filtered water
- ½ C On Guard® Cleaner Concentrate or Castile Soap Natural cleaner concentrate

Instructions

1. Place the package of disposable wipes in a Ziploc bag or reusable plastic container
2. In a bowl, mix the water and cleaner thoroughly
3. Pour your mixture over the wipes and seal
4. You can store these right by your milking area and keep them handy!

When comparing cow's milk to goat's milk, you will find smaller butterfat globules. What this means is that the goat's milk will be more digestible and contain less carotene than cow's milk.

When making products like cheese, goat's milk will produce a softer cheese than that made from cow's milk, even though the butterfat content will be relatively the same.

Homemade Udder Balm

Your does udders are super important when it comes to milk production, and it is essential to keep her teats and udder healthy. That's why it is critical to keep those teats and udders clean, healthy, and soft. Depending upon where you live, your does can become dried out, for instance, in the state of Arizona. This recipe deserves a permanent spot in your milking supplies. Just a note on essential oils, make sure that you are buying 100 percent pure so that it is not contaminated by chemicals.

Ingredients

- ½ C coconut oil
- ¾ C olive oil
- 1 C beeswax
- 1 t raw honey
- 10 drops lavender 100 percent pure essential oil
- 10 drops tea tree 100 percent pure essential oil

Instructions

1. Combine coconut oil, olive oil, and beeswax to the top of a double boiler.
2. Slowly melt these over a low flame, then remove them from the heat
3. When the mixture is warm (not hot), add in your honey and essential oils
4. Chill your mixture in the refrigerator for an hour.

5. Remove the mixture and place it under a mixer to whip for 10 minutes or until the mixture appears fluffy.
6. Place the mixture in a mason jar or clean glass jar to store.

Goat's Milk Composition

Most people assume that since cow's milk doesn't freeze well because of the cream separating after the freezing and thawing process, that you should also resist the practice of freezing goat or sheep's milk, but that's not entirely accurate. Goat and sheep's milk can be frozen for up to 30 days and can be used for drinking. Frozen milk should not be used to make any type of cheese. Also, when you compare goat's milk to cow's milk, you should remember that it is lower in fat, calories, and even lower in cholesterol levels. As a bonus, it provides more calcium. Surprisingly, goat's milk and cheese tend to be easier on the stomach than their cow counterparts. So often, people with digestive issues with cow products may be able to consume the goat version without incident.

The average composition of goat's milk is as follows:

Water	86.0 %
Albuminous Protein	1.0 %
Casein	3.3 %

Lactose	4.4 %
Butterfat	4.5 %
Minerals	0.8 %
Total Solids	14.0%

When making cheese from raw goat's milk, you may find that it will have a distinct peppery hot smell to it that is caused by naturally occurring fatty acids and lipase enzymes.

In any recipe, not goat milk specific, you may want to reduce a recipe's temperature by five degrees since goat's milk curds tend to be more delicate. Always remember that goat curds will need to be treated more gently.

Using Raw Milk

Raw milk is not pasteurized and contains a higher vitamin content than any heat-treated milk. Raw milk embodies the fullness and richness of flavors.

Should you choose to utilize raw milk, you should do so within 48 hours of being milked. If you are pulling milk from your own herd, you should wait at least 2 or 3 hours before using the product.

If you are making cheese with raw milk, please remember to top-stir when you see any butterfat rising to the surface. By doing this, you will mix the butterfat back into the body of the milk.

When using raw milk, it is typically not necessary to add calcium chloride, since the calcium of the milk has not been changed by the pasteurization process or any other long-term cold storage. Since many cheesemakers use calcium chloride in their product to help compensate for any seasonal variations in their collected milk, I still like to use it. It will not hurt your cheese.

There are natural floras contained within your raw milk that can be useful in the making of cheese. However, you should be aware that if you consume and produce products that use raw milk, you should be 100 percent certain that there are no pathogens contaminating the milk.

Raw milk should only come from tested animals that are kept clean and never, under any circumstances, should raw milk be used from an animal suffering from mastitis or receiving antibiotics. Even though raw milk cheeses are some of the best worldwide, make sure that if you are buying or producing raw cheeses, all precautions are being followed on a regular basis.

Top-Stirring

When you top-stir, this action takes place just below the surface of your raw milk. Should you be using raw milk, top-stir it for another 30 seconds when adding rennet. Note: rennet is an enzyme used to set the cheese during the process of making the product. When stirred into a vat of cultured milk, it can cause the mile to separate into solids (curds) and liquid (whey). Rennet can be found at any health food store near you or online.

This will mix any butterfat that has risen to the surface of your product back into the body of the milk. Top-stirring is using the bottom of a slotted spoon to stir the top ¼ of the milk.

Pasteurizing Your Milk at Home

Pasteurized milk goes through a heat treatment to destroy any pathogens. However, it reduces the availability of proteins, vitamins, and milk sugars, in addition to destroying some enzymes. It is a very easy process and can be done on your stove top.

According to Ricki Carroll (2018), if you want to pasteurize your milk at home, just follow these steps:

1. Pour your raw milk product into a double boiler to protect it from becoming scalded.
2. Slowly heat the milk to 145°F (63°C) for precisely 30 minutes while stirring occasionally. The temperature during this cook time must remain constant, so you may find you will need to raise or lower the flame accordingly.
3. Once done, remove the pot of milk from the heat and place it in a sink filled with ice water.

Stir constantly until the temperature of your process drops to 40°F. This step of rapid cooling is important to eliminate any conditions that would support the growth of unwanted bacteria.

4. Store your milk in a sealed container in the refrigerator until you are ready to use it.

How to Make Goat Cheese

Now that you are an expert goat herder and have all the milking processes and handling down pat, you are probably itching to whip up some homemade goat cheeses to impress your family, friends, and neighbors!

It is easy to make cheese at home and one of the great things is that you can flavor them how you want and the best thing of all is that you will know exactly what went into your tasty cheese products.

Even if you are still relatively new to goat herding, milking, and now cheese making, you will be amazed that the process is much simpler than what you have built up in your mind.

This creamy goat cheese that we used as an example uses what is called a coagulation method. What this basically means is that you will combine the goat's milk with heat and acid. By doing this, the ingredients break down into curds and whey. For this simplistic method, you will need no special equipment except for some cheesecloth and a thermometer. You will collect any curds and drain to become cheese - Voilá!

<u>*Equipment*</u>

- A large saucepan
- Measuring cups and spoons
- Cheesecloth
- Thermometer
- Beeswax wrap or cling wrap

<u>*Ingredients*</u>

- 8 ⅓ C Fresh goats milk
- ½ C Water
- 1.5 t citric acid (you can also substitute ⅔ C fresh lemon juice or ½ C vinegar, if you are using lemon or vinegar you will not need to add water)
- 1 t cheese salt (kosher salt)

Optional ingredients:

- Add dried herbs, such as chives, thyme, rosemary, etc. This should be added at the same time as your milk so that it is distributed evenly throughout the cheese
- You can add fresh herbs or chopped nuts to the outside of your cheese log
- Drizzle with honey and a little cinnamon

<u>*Instructions*</u>

1. Prepare your citric acid by dissolving it in water. There will be no need to heat the mixture.
2. Heat your goat's milk by pouring it into a large saucepan. Add the previously dissolved citric

acid and carefully stir. This should be heated slowly and over medium heat until the contents reach 185°F (85°C). When this is achieved, remove the pan from the heat source.

3. Let your milk curdle while it sits aside and rests. Cover it with a lid or tea towel for 10 minutes. You will notice that goat's milk will not curdle in the same manner as cow's milk and the curds will be smaller and less *formed*, which simply means that your mixture will still look like liquid after 10 minutes.

4. Drain the cheese by placing cheesecloth inside of a sieve and pour the milk into the cheesecloth, draining it for about an hour. During this time, you can leave the sieve over a large bowl and collect the leftover whey to use in other recipes that you have in mind.

5. Add the salt to the drained cheese and mix it well. At this time, you will form your cheese by either placing it into a mold or rolling the product into a log. You can easily roll the product into a log by placing it over a piece of beeswax wrap, plastic wrap, or even wax paper, and use these products to form the cheese into a log. Twist or fold in the ends to secure your cheese roll. Move this to your refrigerator to chill and set up. After that, your homemade goat cheese will be ready to eat!

6. Optional: If you want a smoother, creamier cheese, once your product has set, you can

blend it with some water (2-3 T as needed) to produce a smooth and creamy end product.

Goat Milk Cheeses Are Made Worldwide

Goat cheese comes in many different textures and flavors. There are always options to add that can give your cheese a mild or tangy flavor. Goat cheese is versatile and once you make your own, you may find it habit-forming. Below is a list of cheeses that are all made from goat milk:

- Anari cheese
- Añejo cheese
- Anthotyros
- Ardagh castle cheese
- Ardsallagh goat farm
- Banon cheese
- Bastardo del Grappa
- Blue Rathgore
- Bluebell Falls
- Bokmakiri cheese
- Bonne bouche
- Bouq Émissaire
- Brunost
- Bucheron
- Cabécou
- Cabrales cheese
- Caciotta
- Capricious
- Caprino cheese

- Caprino dell'Aspromonte
- Castelo Branco cheese
- Cathare
- Chabichou
- Chabis
- Chaubier
- Chavroux
- Chèvre noir
- Chevrotin
- Circassian cheese
- Circassian smoked cheese
- Clochette
- Clonmore cheese
- Cooleeney Farmhouse cheese
- Corleggy cheese
- Couronne lochoise
- Crottin de Chavignol
- Dolaz cheese
- Faisselle
- Feta
- Formaela
- Garrotxa cheese
- Gbejna friska
- Gbejna tal bzar
- Gbejna mghoxxa
- Geitost
- Gevrik
- Dunlop cheese
- Gleann Gabhra
- Glyde Farm Produce

- Graviera
- Halloumi
- Harbourne blue
- Humboldt Fog
- Jibneh Arabieh
- Kars Gravyer cheese
- Kasseri
- Kefalotyri
- Kunik cheese
- Leipäjuusto
- Majorero
- Manouri
- Mató
- Mizithra
- Nabulsi cheese
- Pantysgawn
- Payoyo cheese
- Pélardon
- Picodon
- Picón Bejes-Tresviso
- Pouligny-Saint-Pierre cheese
- Queso Palmita
- Rigotte de Condrieu
- Robiola
- Rocamadour cheese
- Rubing
- Sainte-Maure de Touraine
- Santarém cheese
- Selles-sur-Cher cheese
- Snøfrisk

- St Helen's
- St Tola
- Testouri
- Tesyn
- Tulum cheese
- Valençay cheese
- Van herbed cheese
- Xynomizithra
- Xynotyro

According to Analida (2021), the use of goat cheese and goat milk dates back to the fifth millenium BC, when goats were kept by shepherds and herders. Goat cheese even made an appearance in Greek mythology, set in Homer's epic tale The Odyssey. Even ancient Egyptian tombs depict cheese-making drawings. By the rise of the Roman Empire, cheese-making was a well-established practice.

Recipes

Soft Goat Cheese

Ingredients

- 1 gallon goat's milk
- ½ t calcium chloride, diluted in ¾ C of cool non-chlorinated water
- 1 packet buttermilk direct-set culture
- 1 drop liquid rennet diluted in 5 tablespoons of cool non-chlorinated water
- 1 t cheese salt (optional)

Instructions

1. Heat your milk to 86°F (30°C) and add the calcium chloride solution. Stir well. Sprinkle the buttermilk starter over the surface of the milk, then wait 2 minutes for the powder to rehydrate. Stir well to combine.
2. Next, add the diluted rennet solution and gently stir the mixture with an up and down motion for a total of 30 seconds.
3. Cover and allow the milk solution to set at 72°F (22°C) during a time frame of 12-24 hours or until you notice firm coagulation.

4. Place 4 to 8 soft-cheese molds on top of a draining mat and then set on a wire rack set up over a basin to collect your whey.

5. Gently ladle the curds into the molds, taking care to not break up the curd.

6. Fill the molds and wait 15 minutes for the curd to settle, then ladle more curd into the molds until the mixture is completely used up. Allow the cheese to drain for 18-24 hours. During that time, turn once to help with drainage. The final result will settle by one-third to one-half of its original amount.

7. Unmold your cheese. If desired, you can take the optional salt and sprinkle it lightly after unmolding. You are now ready to eat the finished product, or wrap it up in a cheese wrap and store it for up to 2 weeks in your refrigerator.

Goat's Milk Cheddar

Ingredients

- 2 gallons of goat's milk
- ½ t calcium chloride diluted in ¼ C cool non-chlorinated water
- 1 packet direct-set mesophilic starter culture
- ½ t liquid rennet diluted in ¼ C cool non-chlorinated water
- 2 T plus 1 t cheese salt

- Cheese wax (optional)

Instructions

1. Heat the milk to 85°F (29°C) and add the calcium chloride solution. Stir well to combine ingredients. Sprinkle the starter over the surface of the milk mixture and wait 2 minutes for the power to rehydrate. Stir well, then cover and allow the milk to ripen for 30 minutes.

2. Next, add the diluted rennet and stir gently with an up and down motion for a total of 30 seconds. Cover the pot holding the mixture and let it set for 1 hour at 85°F (29°C).

3. Cut the curd into ½-inch cubes and allow them to sit undisturbed for 10 minutes.

4. Gradually heat these curds 2 degrees every 5 minutes until they are 98°F (37°C). Stir gently every 3 minutes to prevent the curds from matting. Maintain this temperature for 45 minutes while stirring gently every 3 minutes.

5. Remove the whey and add 2 tablespoons of the salt to the curds and then mix.

6. Line a 2 pound cheese mold with cheesecloth and ladle the curds into the mold. You will need to press the cheese at 20 pounds of pressure for 15 minutes.

7. Remove the cheese from the mold and gently peel away the cheesecloth, then flip the cheese,

rewrap it, then place it back into the mold. Press at 30 pounds of pressure for about an hour.

8. Unwrap. Flip. Rewrap and press at 50 pounds of pressure for 12 hours. At this point, you can remove the press and gently peel away the cheesecloth. Rub salt on all the surfaces, then place it on a cheeseboard.

9. For the next 2 days, turn your cheese once daily while rubbing salt on it once a day at room temperature. When the surface is dry, you can wax it to create a moister cheese or age it for something drier.

10. Age the cheese at 50-55°F (10-13°C) for 4-12 weeks

Dry Cottage Cheese

Ingredients

- 1 gallon goat's milk
- ¼ t calcium chloride, diluted in ¼ cup of cool non-chlorinated water
- 1 packet chèvre starter culture or 1 packet direct set buttermilk starter culture
- 3 drops liquid rennet, diluted in ¼ c of cool non-chlorinated water (use this only if using the buttermilk starter culture).
- Cheese salt (optional)
- Herbs (optional)

Instructions

1. Heat the milk to 72°F (23°C), then add the calcium chloride solution. Stir well to combine the ingredients, then sprinkle the starter over the surface of the mixture. Wait 2 minutes until the powder rehydrates. Stir well.

2. If you are using the buttermilk starter instead of the chèvre starter, then add the rennet solution and stir gently with an up and down motion for a total of 30 seconds. (If you have used the chèvre starter, then skip all of these instructions.)

3. Cover the mixture and let it set at 72°F (23°C) for 24 hours.

4. Cut the curd into ½ inch cubes and allow them to rest for 5 minutes.

5. Gradually heat these curds to 116°F (47°C) by raising the temperature 5 degrees every 5 minutes for 40 minutes. Stir every 3 minutes to prevent the curds from matting.

6. Allow your curds to rest for 5 minutes at 116°F (47°C). When the curd is ready, it will be slightly resistant when pressed between your fingers.

7. Remove the butter muslin and submerge the colander of curd in a pot of cold, sterilized water in order to remove the lactose from the curds. When the water appears to be milky, then drain it off and replace it. You are ready to drain and store the cheese when the water runs clear.

You can put this in your refrigerator for up to 10 days.

8. Should you want to add salt or herbs to boost the taste, mix these in just before eating.

Goat Milk Vanilla Ice Cream

<u>*Ingredients*</u>

- 3 large, whole eggs
- 2 ounces fresh goat cheese (chevre) preferably smooth and spreadable
- ½ C sugar
- 6 T dry, full-fat goat milk powder
- Pinch of salt
- 2 C whole goat milk
- 1 T tapioca syrup
- 2 t vanilla extract

Goat Milk Chocolate Ice Cream

<u>*Ingredients*</u>

- 3 large, whole eggs
- 2 ounces fresh goat cheese (chevre) preferably smooth and spreadable
- ½ C sugar
- 3 T Dutch process cocoa powder
- 6 T full fat, dry goat milk powder
- ⅛ t salt

- 2 C whole goat milk
- 2 T tapioca syrup
- 1 t vanilla extract

Instructions for Either Ice Cream

1. In a medium-sized bowl, whisk the eggs until yolks and whites are combined. Set them aside.
2. In a small bowl, warm the goat cheese until soft and whisk it until smooth. Set this aside too.
3. For the chocolate ice cream only: whisk together the dry ingredients until the mixture is free of lumps. Set aside.
4. Add the 2 cups of milk and tapioca syrup to a 3 or 4-quart saucepan. Heat this over medium-high heat. Stir frequently until the ingredients reach a simmer.
5. Add the dry ingredients (vanilla or chocolate) to the hot milk and whisk this until dissolved. Remove the mixture from the heat source.
6. Add a generous portion of the hot milk mixture by drizzling it into the eggs. Whisk briskly while adding.
7. Now, carefully pour the egg mixture into the saucepan with the balance of the hot milk. This should be done while continuing to whisk the milk.
8. Cook this over medium-low heat and stir constantly, if possible with a heat-proof spatula, but if you do not have one, a spoon will

suffice). Scrape all portions of the bottom of the pan until the mixture thickens and reaches a temperature of 170-175°F. It should appear thicker than uncooked milk, and this process should take about 7-14 minutes. Remove mixture from the heat.

9. You will gradually add some of the hot custard into the softened cheese (about ½ cup to a cup). Whisk after each addition until the mixture is smooth.

10. Pour the cheese mixture into the saucepan and continue to whisk until combined.

11. Pour through a fine-mesh strainer and into a clean bowl.

12. Cool in a cold water bath for about 30 minutes, or if you want, you can place the mixture directly into the refrigerator. Stir occasionally during those first 30 minutes of cooling.

13. Cool completely, which would be a minimum of 4 hours, but preferable to be overnight.

14. Stir in the vanilla extract, then churn in an ice cream maker following any manufacturer instructions for the equipment.

15. Transfer the contents to a 1-quart freezer storage container. At this time, you can stir in any desired additions you wish.

16. Store in your freezer and enjoy!

Goat Milk Candles

Equipment and Ingredients

- Beeswax
- Double boiler
- Goat's milk
- Vanilla 100 percent pure essential oil
- Wick
- Scissors

Instructions

1. Place 2 lbs of beeswax into the top of a double boiler and heat the water in the bottom over high heat until the wax melts.
2. Add ¼ cup of goat's milk into the wax and stir this thoroughly with a spoon until both are combined, and the ingredients bind together.
3. Add any scents to the mixture, for example, the vanilla essential oil. Use only pure essential oils, as cheaper blends contain chemicals that may be toxic to burn.
4. Cut wicks at least two inches longer than your desired candle height. If you want, you can tie a metal washer to the end of one side of the wick.
5. Either way, you lift the wick out of the wax and hold it in the air. Once the wax has begun to solidify, you can dip it back into the wax. Remove it after it's been covered. Repeat these steps until the candle reaches your desired thickness.
6. Once you have reached this stage, place your candles on a sheet of newspaper until they become completely cooled.
7. You can give candles to friends, decorate your home, even make them to sell for charitable events.

Frequently Asked Questions

When making recipes, we all have questions regarding the making of cheese products. Here are a few common questions and some sensible answers.

- **Why did my cheese turn out crumbly?** The milk may have been heated too quickly. Try heating your mixture slower because that is the key.

- **What kind of vinegar should I use?** White vinegar.

- **What type of milk can I use?** Use a fat-type milk and avoid the use of anything ultra-pasteurized because the high heat will affect the proteins, and you will notice that the curds will not form well. You should always use the freshest milk possible.

- **Can I rinse my curds before storing them?** Yes. Gently rinsing your curds will remove some of the tangy flavors of the acid you used to coagulate the milk. It all depends on the taste you desire. Stir in any salts and herbs after the rinsing procedure.

Chapter 4:

The BEST Meat

Without a doubt, the highest cost of raising meat goats is the feeding program. Any animal that is raised for meat requires a high level of nutrients that support meat production.

Where goats differ from cattle or sheep is their ratio of weight gain and if you are new to the management of goats for meat then you should be aware that they do not fatten like sheep or cattle. The general ratios of meat goats range from between 0.1 to 0.8 lbs per day.

In order to achieve a profit, they must be fed a high-quality forage and often be supplemented with an expensive, but effective concentrated feed. (A concentrated feed will generally have higher nutrients packed into a pellet where the feed ratio is less than other feeds.)

If you have exposure to other people who also raise goats for meat, perhaps they will share some of their philosophies on their year-round forage program. Most of these will include as much grazing as possible throughout the year.

There are people trying to raise meat goats that honestly believe a low-quality feed is sufficient, but keep in mind that you have to feed muscle to make muscle and if you are a human athlete, ask yourself the following question: can I compete in a triathlon with a diet of junk food? I am sure that you already know the answer to that question!

Feeding Requirements

You may have some previous experience with cattle, but a goat does not digest plants as well as a cow. The reason for this is that the feed stays in a goat's rumen for a shorter period of time. There is also a distinction between what forage will work best for your animals. While trees and shrubs do not provide quality roughage for a cow, the same cannot be said for your goat herd. A cow might graze through some straw and be able to use some of that low protein that it offers, but straw will not even provide nutritional maintenance in a goat. Why? Simply, because goats do not use the cell wall of straw as effectively as a cow.

Another reason that goats should consume a higher quality diet is due to the size of their digestive tract. It is considerably smaller, but in relation to their body weight, the amount of feed needed by meat goats is almost twice that of cattle.

Nutrient Requirements

Protein, minerals, and vitamins, along with water are all essential in the nutritional needs of your meat goats. Without these critical nutrients, it will be difficult for your meat goats to remain in good flesh, be able to reproduce, support a pregnancy, or support the production of meat, milk, or hair.

In a pasture, your animals will have access to lush leafy forage, but during winter months or in times of drought, you will have to provide the highest quality hay you can find. You should always have your hay and pasture tested annually to know what nutrients you can count on. Just because your pasture was lush last year, the following year is a whole new growing season and the nutritional content can be affected by many things, such as too much rain, too little rain, or even an invasive insect. No two growing years are going to be exactly the same.

No matter if your goats are grazed, barn fed, or a combination of the two, your animals should be offered a supplemental concentrated feed to cover any nutritional deficiencies in your grazing program.

Total digestible nutrients (TDN) will give you an idea of where your forage will fall in regard to its nutritional content. Below is a chart that reflects the daily nutrient requirements for feeding your meat-producing goats provided by NC State Extensions (2015).

- Low-quality forages are 40-55 % TDN
- Good quality forages are between 55-70% TDN

Daily	Yo		Doe				Buc

Nutrient Requirements for Meat Producing Goats	ung Goats		s (110 lb)				ks (80 - 120 lb)
Nutrient	Weanling (30 lb)	Yearling (60 lb)	Pregnant (early)	Pregnant (late)	Lactating (avg milk)	Lactating (high milk)	
Dry Matter, lb	2.0	3.0	4.5	4.5	4.5	5.0	5.0
TDN. %	68	65	55	60	60	65	60
Protein, %	14	12	10	11	11	14	11
Calcium, %	.6	.4	.4	.4	.4	.6	.4

Phosphorus, %	.3	.2	.2	.2	.2	.3	.2

Protein

The attainment of your protein levels will be the most expensive part of your goat's diet. You will find protein in lush, leafy forage, tree leaves, hay, and grains. Feed grains provide high protein by using whole cottonseed, soybean meal, wheat middlings, and corn gluten. Proteins are required and provide a source of nitrogen for the ruminal bacteria and needed amino acids to build muscle, bone integrity, and how the muscles adhere to the bone.

When levels of protein run low in your animal's diet, their digestion of carbohydrates in the rumen will slow down and their intake of feed will decrease. In a domino effect, this will continue to lower your levels of proteins in your animal's diet and will, in turn, affect your animal's growth rate, milk production, reproduction, and the ability to fight off diseases. You do not need to worry about extra protein being stored in your goat's body because any excess will be excreted out in their urine.

Proper amounts of protein are vital to cover your herd's nutritional needs.

Minerals

Goats, like all other members of the animal kingdom, need minerals to support basic body function. A free choice complete goat-specific loose mineral mix will cover any major minerals that are likely to be deficient in your herd's diet. Chelated minerals are always a better choice as they are more bioavailable for your animals. The major minerals these typically cover are:

- Sodium chloride (salt)
- Calcium
- Phosphorous
- Magnesium
- Selenium
- Copper
- **Zinc**

Calcium to phosphorus ratios in any animal's diet is important and for your goats, they should be kept in the 2:1 - 3:1 ratio.

Depending upon which area of the country you live in, your soil may be deficient in selenium. Predominantly North Carolina and most of the Southeast are the areas most affected by this deficiency and for that reason, many commercialized trace mineral salts do not contain selenium. For your herd, you should provide trace mineral salts that do include selenium.

While goats tend to accept copper more readily than sheep, you should be aware that young, nursing kids are more sensitive to copper toxicity than their grown fellow herd members. For this reason, you should never feed cattle milk replacers to nursing kids. It is also worth mentioning that the maximum copper level for a goat to tolerate has never been established. Therefore, you should always use caution when choosing proper supplementation for your goats.

Vitamins

We all need vitamins, and your goats are no different. Because of their size, most will be needed in very small quantities. The vitamins that your herd may be deficient in are A and D.

Because a goat's rumen will form bacteria responsible for all B and K vitamins, these are not essential vitamins required in goat nutrition. Vitamin C needs are met by the synthesized quantities made within your goat's body tissues.

Those green, leafy forage pieces that your goat consumes contain carotene, which their bodies convert into vitamin A. Goats are also capable of storing vitamin A in their liver and fat when they consume more than needed. If, however, your goat is not taking in sufficient vitamin A, they will need support for that vitamin level.

If your herd is confined in barns for long periods during the winter, they should still have access to frequent sunlight. This exposure creates vitamin D to be produced under their skin. If not, they will need to receive supplemental vitamin D. Good quality sun-cured hay can be a good source for your animals to intake vitamin D. When an animal experiences a deficiency in vitamin D, they will not be able to absorb calcium and this can lead to an animal developing rickets (this is a condition where young animals or even people will grow abnormally in their bones and joints).

Water

Water is the life force for every living creature. It is necessary and the cheapest of your feed ingredients. Your lactating does should always have access to high-quality water. Always provide fresh, clean water for your herd. Always have your water tested to make sure that there are no unhealthy levels of nitrate in your properties drinking water.

Tip: A smaller water container is easier to maintain, keeping the water clean and fresh for your herd. This will require changing and refilling more often.

Energy

Your animal's energies come from carbohydrates found in sugars, starches, fats, and fibers in their diet. If your herd is struggling with finding sufficient sources of energy, then you might want to add a grain that will provide for the deficiency. Grains that are high in energy contain whole cottonseed, corn, wheat middlings, soybean hulls, soybean meal, and corn gluten. Any added fat should not represent more than 5 percent of your animal's diet. If it ends up representing too much of your animal's diet, that extra fat will be stored in your goat's body around many of their internal organs.

Which Are the BEST Meat Goats?

Frankly, goats from any number of breeds end up getting slaughtered for their meat. However, not every breed is bred specifically for meat production. The one breed that stands out more than the rest is the Boer, which is a breed best known by the people living in the Upper Midwest of the United States associated with meat production. Developed in South Africa, the Boer is one of the few breeds selectively bred for meat harvesting. Incredibly, the Boer is a newer addition to the United States and was first imported in 1993 from New Zealand.

Other goat breeds that are generally acknowledged as meat producers are Spanish, Pygmy, Kiko, and the Myotonic (fainting goat).

Even if you primarily raise dairy goats, sooner or later, most owners will decide to cull the herd's least productive animals. Those targeted will be low milk producers, poor mothers, and the least valuable of the newest bunch of kids. Especially if you are a dairy producer, you may want to consider culling if you have had a bumper crop of male kids because typically, you only keep one out of every 100 bucks in the eventuality that you need to replace an aging patriarch buck.

Navigating the Goat Meat Industry

Meat goat production usually includes the owning, breeding, raising, and selling of your animals and does not always mean that you will be processing the animals as well. You can become involved by raising them and caring for them until their time of sale.

You can get started by purchasing several does, getting them bred by your buck, a buck you have leased, or AI (artificial insemination). You will care for your does all through their pregnancy and make nutritional decisions. When their kids are delivered, you will care for them until their time of sale. The production of these animals is a year-round commitment, and you should establish a budget for how and where your investment monies will be spent, especially when just getting started.

Just like any business, you will need to know where your animals will be sold. Because the meat goat industry is fairly new, it might be difficult to find the best place to sell your animals right away. This can be frustrating for beginners to navigate through leads in order to find your best market. You should develop a marketing plan that details your targets.

Regional Auction Market

This is typically an auction barn that will sell goats for you, the producer.

- **Advantages**

- o   There is no need for you to find buyers.
- **Disadvantages**
  - o   This type of market can be unpredictable, causing you to lose money or break even.
  - o   You, as the seller, will have to pay a percentage of the final price to the auction barn as a commission.
  - o   Depending upon the auction house, or the sale, your goats might be sold by the pound instead of a per animal basis. This can make it difficult to determine what the most profitable animals are to produce.

Niche Markets

These are markets developed by you, the producer, and others like you to reach a specific demand. Perhaps a country farmer's market type of event.

- **Advantages**
  - o   The producer (you), can obtain better value.
  - o   The customer base can become regulars, and they are looking for specifics.
  - o   The product you offer is well-defined.
- **Disadvantages**
  - o   These types of markets can be seasonal, so you cannot count on them for year-round support.

○ You become dependent upon the demands shaped by the customer base, and you are subject to their current needs.

○ You will need to work hard to market and maintain your market to ensure any levels of success.

○ These are markets developed by you, the producer, and others like you to reach a specific demand. Perhaps a country farmer's market type of event.

Seedstock Markets

This particular market will involve the selling of high-quality breeding animals.

- **Advantages**
  ○ The type of market will allow you as a producer to capture more value for your high-end replacement breeding animals.
- **Disadvantages**
  ○ To survive in this market, you will have to survive trends in the breeding industry and popular opinions.
  ○ This outlet is only for animals that are quality enough to be used as breeding stock, and therefore not a good choice for marketing the majority of your herd that is for sale.

Show Prospect Markets

This market targets only the show industry. However, this can provide a name for your farm.

- **Advantages**
    - Prices tend to remain stable
    - Goats shown in different ranges of shows will provide publicity for your farm and your brand.
- **Disadvantages**
    - This is only an outlet for the goats you have bred that are of a high enough quality to be competitive in the show ring.
    - Just as with any show ring featuring animals, this makes your sales prospects subject to any trends and cycles in the industry. This makes it necessary for you to keep up with what is trending and keep your quality goats in high demand.

Youth Livestock Sales

This market is solely for goats that are exhibited in youth shows.

- **Advantages**
    - The market is well established.

- ○ Sellers tend to receive a premium over the market value.
- **Disadvantages**
  - ○ Buyers may be limited in this market.
  - ○ The seller must find their own buyers, typically.
  - ○ There is no guarantee that your animal will be accepted into the sale.

Keep Records

You are going to want to keep track of your successes and failures in order to decide what methods work the best for you and to weed out any methods that don't produce the desired results. It doesn't matter which goat type of business you pursue, but records are the only way for you to keep track of your expenses and keep track of what methods and outlets are working for you. Make sure that you record all useful information, no matter how small it might be.

Keep your record-keeping methods easy and simple to understand so that when you revisit them, there will be no confusion.

Here are some things we recommend keeping track of:

- Expenses
- Income
- Animal Inventory
- Feeding Records

- Animal Health Records
- Emergency Vet Care
- Breeding Records
- Birthing Records
- Weaning Rates
- Weight Gain Chart
- Goals

Breeding and Raising Your Flock

Just like anything you create, you want to start with the correct quality ingredients. While it may take time to develop your intuition about the selection of your breeding stock, learning the fundamentals will only help you in the end. Never be afraid to ask questions of anyone that you feel can give you excellent tips and advice.

Picking Your Breeds

While it's true that all goats can be harvested for their meat, there are certain breeds that are more predisposed for top meat production. For that reason, you should always make the best decisions possible when choosing your breeding stock. Top chosen breeds include:

- **Boer** - This breed excels as a meat producer and carries a high fertility and growth rate.

- **Spanish** - Are known to be breedable, even when outside of the typical breeding season. Their appeal is that they are very hardy and do well in difficult environments. With some recent changes in breeding toward better meat production within this breed, they have increased in suitability to sustain a goat meat herd.
- **New Zealand Kiko** - This breed is a result of crossbreeding heavier muscled wild does with Saanen and Nubian bucks. The end result was developing this breed to be a larger framed animal that is capable of early maturing.
- **Tennessee Fainting Goat** - Besides exhibiting the condition called myotonia, these goats have the ability to breed out of season and will kid up to twice each year. They are chosen for meat breeding production because they tend to be a very muscular animal.

The above breeds are not your only choices for meat production, but we have mentioned them because they are most suited to drive a farm's meat production business. When you start to do your research, you will find that there are further crossbreeds to consider using these breeds and certain dairy goats that ramp up meat production. Your location may be a deciding factor on which goat breeds you think will work best for you.

If you are purchasing your foundation herd, you should probably take age into your equation. If you are looking to build your kid crop right away, you should purchase goats that will be old enough to breed. Males will reach their breeding capabilities between 4 and 8 months of age, while females tend to age a bit slower, and they are ready for breeding between 7 and 10 months. These ages can vary between breeds, so do your research before making your final decisions. Many producers tend to hold off breeding during their first year, preferring instead to let their animals mature during their first year, so their bodies are better able to withstand the demands of pregnancy.

Evaluation

It can take practice to become knowledgeable enough to make practiced decisions when it comes to evaluating your potential livestock additions. The goats you choose for your herd will have a direct impact on your end breeding results. You can be the best manager in the world and show infallible instinct regarding the running of y0ur operation, but the bottom line is that you need to begin with good livestock.

There are many people out there that have excellent track records regarding the development of a great meat-producing herd, and most of them are willing to help out a greenhorn. They will use terms like condition or finish, which indicates the amount of fat covering the spine and ribs. When more knowledgeable people use terms like style or balance, this refers to growth, appeal, production, or muscle. When an animal has style, they have an appealing look that will catch a buyer's attention. A female should appear to have a long, thin neck, a smooth shoulder line, and be more refined than a male. Within the same breed, a buck should appear more masculine and have a heavier bone structure.

There can be a fine line regarding weight for your market animal because a thin layer of fat is necessary to produce a more tender, and fresher selection of meats, whereas too much fat will make the meat unappealing to potential customers.

Take time to study a goat's body structure to enable you to better understand the evaluation process. The biggest problem areas of confirmation are the shoulder, pasterns, and hip areas and these can impact your herd ideal. Problems that are apparent when the animal is younger will only worsen with age, making it difficult to keep your animals producing for many years to come. You should always select animals that are heavily muscled to develop a more production-oriented herd. Obviously, the muscles that produce the most meat are the most important to focus on (These would be the shoulder, leg, and loin).

Tip: Goats that are better muscled generally stand and walk wider. Also, when attempting to evaluate a potential animal, muscle creates a goat's shape and the fat should be smooth and flat.

Here are some helpful hints when learning to evaluate your potential animal's structure:

- The animal's top and bottom jaws should align. Over or underbites are not a desirable trait.

- Shoulders should demonstrate a 45-degree angle.
- The goat's topline should be mostly level and not appear tented.
- The angle from hooks to pins (you can discover these by viewing a goat's skeletal structure) should seem to be gently sloping.
- The animal's hock should display enough angle to allow for easy movement.
- All four pasterns should demonstrate a 45-degree angle.

Chapter 5:

Fiber for the Win

If you are new to the fiber industry, you may not be aware that this industry has been in existence for over 100 years. Unfortunately, the fiber industry has seen some recent struggles in regards to the amount of product available because many producers of fiber have either changed breeds or products. Today, efforts are being made to regrow some of the recent losses of producers.

Especially if this is your first time as a goat owner, you should start small with your fiber business and not overwhelm yourself with everything you need to know and a huge herd that might make you feel pressured. Joining local and national fiber goat organizations is one of the best ways to get started in the ownership of fiber goats. By doing this, you can meet others involved in the industry that have more experience than yourself.

Fiber Goat Associations and Registries

We want to provide you with a list of possible organizations you may want to look into:

- American Angora Goat Breeders Association (AAGBA)
- American Colored Angora Goat Registry
- American Nigora Goat Breeders Association
- Australian Cashmere Growers Association
- Cashmere Goat Association
- Colored Angora Goat Breeders Association (CAGBA)
- Eastern Angora Goat & Mohair Association (EAGMA)
- Cashmere and Camel Hair Manufacturers Institute (CCMI)
- Northwest Cashmere Association
- American Goat Federation (AGF)
- Pygora Breeders Association (PBA)
- The Angora Goat Society (U.K.)
- Miniature Silky Fainting Goat Association (MSFGA)

In chapter 1, we briefly introduced you to the best choices of goats to buy when pursuing a fiber goat herd. Let's briefly revisit those breeds:

- Angora goat's origins date back to early biblical history. These goats are sheared twice a year before breeding (Fall) and before kidding

(Spring). They are a bit unusual because both sexes display horns, but they are best known for their long, wavy hair and their relaxed and docile nature.

Meeting the nutritional needs of the angora goats will be a producer's main concern since these goats have very high nutrient requirements.

Tip: When your does kid, they should be moved into stalls. Kids that are cold will not suck, and they may require a heat lamp. The Angora does and kids should be left as undisturbed as possible for several weeks because does have a tendency to abandon their kids.

- Cashmere goats have been bred selectively to produce a more significant amount of cashmere fiber. The truth is that any goat grows cashmere because that is the goat's soft undercoat. It should be noted that the American cashmere industry has very high standards regarding the quality of any cashmere fiber. Raising healthy animals is a good start to maintaining the quality needed. Cashmere goats are described as being flighty and high-strung. Cashmere breeds are:
  - Australian Cashmere goat
  - Changthangi (Kashmir Pashmina Cashmere goat
  - Hexi
  - Inner Mongolia Cashmere goat
  - Liaoning Cashmere goat

- Licheng Daqing goat
- Luliang black goat
- Tibetan Plateau goat
- Wuzhumuqin
- Zalaa Jinst White goat
- Zhongwei Cashmere goat

- There are several various crossbred goats with no specific name. Generally, Angoras can be crossed with many different breeds. Depending on the goat you choose, there can be significantly less fiber availability, so before you jump into cross-breeding, do your homework.

- Nigora goats are a smaller breed of goat and created from breeding a Nigerian Dwarf buck with Angora does. The breeding of these goats began in 1994. They have calm temperaments and also make excellent pets.

- Pygora goats are a cross of a registered Pygmy goat with a registered Angora goat. This is a relatively new breed, established in 1987. They are easy to handle and considered to be good-natured.

All About Shearing

Each breed of goat may have some specifics to follow when shearing, and some breeds will need periodic combing during the year. You will be able to determine this by speaking with other fiber farmers, visiting your breed association, or studying up on your breed or breeds within your herd. Not all goats will have the same shearing requirements. For example, you don't shear a cashmere-producing goat. The process is achieved by combing or plucking the fiber once a year.

If you are practiced, you can shear an animal in 1 to 3 minutes. However, when you are just starting out, you will need to practice, practice, practice. It can be tough and dirty work, and experts say that this is not a job for anyone with a temper.

The general care of your fiber goats is going to be very similar to that of your dairy and meat goats. Without good nutrition, you will not get a good coat on your animals and that is the most important thing you need in order to provide quality fibers. Fiber goats will need extra fats in their diet to help provide the lanolin necessary to protect their coats. You can achieve this by adding some black oil sunflower seeds to their high-end hay and commercial feed. Even adding a little beet pulp can prove beneficial, and it can be fed dry or soaked to provide some extra calories. Should you soak your beet pulp, you can factor in that this will be giving your goats extra water intake, so don't panic if they drink a little less.

General Shearing Tips

- A clean animal is going to be much easier to shear than an animal that is dirty. The dirt will collect in your clippers and dull your blades.
- Prepare your goats for shearing by performing the following:
  - During the few weeks before shearing, you should use a pour-on insecticide that contains either permethrin or pyrethrin to kill any existing lice or ticks.
  - If you are due for rain or show, you should keep your animals confined inside for 24 hours prior to shearing, so they remain dry.
  - Clean and add new bedding to your dry shelter for the time following your shearing process. After being shorn, your herd is more susceptible to health issues due to losing their protective coats.
- Your goats should always be completely dry for the shearing process.
- For beginners, clipping is much easier to perform than shearing.
- It is advised that you not cut the same area twice, so you are only offering the higher quality product.
- When shearing, use long, smooth strokes because this keeps the goat's *fleece* in longer

pieces. Not only will this make the piece easier to work with, but its value will be higher.

- Take care when shearing so that you do not cut their skin. Be extra careful on their belly area, areas where the body meets the legs, and the scrotum and teats. Accidents always happen, but if you do happen to cut one of your goats during the shearing process, you can treat it with antibiotic spray.

- Begin with the youngest goats and work your way through the herd based upon their age, since the youngest usually has the best fiber to offer.

- Shearing isn't necessarily difficult to do, but it can be very hard on the back because of all the time you spent bent over. If you have a bad back, you may want to hire someone to do this step for you.

- If you only have a couple of goats, you can probably perform the shearing with scissors or a pair of hand shears, but if you can afford it and want to perform this action yourself, you can always invest in some electric shears. These will range in price starting at 300.00 dollars and up.

- Gather up these supplies to help you shear:
    ○ Blow-dryer
    ○ Sheep shears
    ○ Grooming stand or stanchion
    ○ Scissors

- ○ Clean paper bags, pillowcases, or even baskets to hold the fiber
- ○ A hanging scale to weigh the fiber

Ready, Set, Shear!

1. Secure your first goat on the grooming stand.
2. Use your blow-dryer on your goat and get rid of any hay, loose hairs, or other pieces of debris that may be in your goat's coat.
3. Shear the goat's belly by starting at the bottom of the chest and move back toward its udder or scrotal area.
4. Shear both sides by working from the belly up to the spine and back leg to the front leg.
5. Shear each hind leg by working from the beginning of the coat, traveling upward toward the spine.
6. Your next step is to shear the neck. Begin at the bottom of the goat's throat and work toward the top of the chest and then on to the ears on the top and sides.
7. By working from the crown of the head and traveling back toward the tail, you will shear the top of the animal's back.
8. Go back and remove any excess hair that you might have missed with your scissors. One area often overlooked is the area of the udder or testicles.

9. Give your goat a treat and release your animal to frolic.

10. Go through your fiber and separate out any stained or soiled particles. Weigh any unsoiled product, then roll it up and put it in a paper bag. Make sure that you mark each bag with the goat's name, their age, the date sheared, and the weight of the product. Store in a dry area.

11. Thoroughly sweep your area so that the next goat will start with a clean environment.

Finding a Shearer

Generally, someone that shears sheep will also be able to shear your goats as well. Remember that if you are not doing your own shearing, to include this in your business expenses.

Fiber Goat Terminology for Beginners

It doesn't matter if you are getting a job in a new industry or getting invested in a new hobby. There are always buzz words or terminology that pertain to that interest. Try to make yourself familiar with these terms, so when you are talking with others, you have a better understanding.

- **Angora Goat** - is a breed of goat that produces mohair.

- **Angora Wool** - this is a textile that actually comes from Angora rabbits, not goats. The only fibers that come from goats are Cashgora, Cashmere, and Mohair.
- **Cashgora** - is a high-quality goat fiber that lies somewhere between Angora fibers and Cashmere fibers. Cashgora goats are cross-bred goats between Angora and Cashmere goats.
- **Cashmere** - This product can come from any goat that grows a quality downy undercoat in the winter. This textile is noted for its softness and warmth.
- **Fiber Goat** - This is a general term for any goat that produces Mohair, Cashmere, or Cashgora.
- **Goat Fiber** - There are several stages of fiber:
    - Raw is what is combed out of the goat's coat before any processing occurs.
    - Processed fiber has been washed, and carded.
    - Virgin fiber has been made into yarns.
    - Recycled fibers are reclaimed from scraps or fabrics.
- **Guard Hairs** - This hair stays all year long and grows through the undercoat; remaining even when the undercoat molts or is combed out.
- **Mohair** - A fleece and silky fiber that is created from the long hair of the Angora goat. Mohair is found in a number of textile products, including yarns for handcrafted products and fabrics.

Chapter 6:

General Health & Diseases

Prevention is key when developing a health program for your herd. You should always practice being observant, and often you can notice the start of any illness before it has a chance to become serious.

Be familiar with diseases common to goats and by using prevention. You can head off most problems before they get a foothold in your herd. It can be as simple as giving each of your animals a once over every morning or evening.

Normal Goat Health Data

Temperature:	104 ∓ 1°F, 40°C
Heart Rate:	70 to 80 beats per minute, faster for kids
Respiration Rate:	12 to 15 breaths per minute, faster for kids
Rumen Movements:	1 to 1.5 contractions per minute

There are some signs to look for when checking your animals, and they include:

- Poor appetite
- Diarrhea
- Limping
- Labored breathing
- Grunting or groaning
- Grinding teeth
- Behavior that is out of character for that animal

When conversing with your veterinarian, it is important that you be as precise as possible and use correct body parts when possible if describing a wound or a limp. When you first acquire your herd, you should question your vet about any common diseases common to your locale.

1. Observe the animal in question from a distance. Jot down their overall condition and age. When making further notes, your checklist can include things like its ability to stand. Is it able to walk normally? Is it staggering or bumping into objects? Does it appear to be able to see? Does it appear to be bloated or exhibit targeted area swelling? If you are able to, can you count the respirations per minute?

2. If you have a helper, they should hold the goat for you to check over. Avoid making the animal run as this can cause false readings regarding pulse, respiratory, and temperature.

3. With a digital thermometer, insert it into the goat's rectum and leave it there for 3 minutes. Make notes on the reading.

4. Place your fingertips, or palm, on the left flank and feel for any rumen movement. Always relay to the vet if your goat reacts in pain, the rumen feels mushy or appears to be filled with water.

5. Place your fingertips on both sides of the lower rib cage and feel for a heart rate, count the heartbeats that take place for one minute, and make a record of it. Your goat's pulse can also be taken by feeling the large artery in the inside of the upper rear leg.

6. You can pull back the lips of your goat's mouth to check the color of the animal's mucous membranes. Pink is the norm unless the

animal's dark skin colors naturally extend into the areas of the mouth.

7. Gently run your hands over the animal's body to search for any swelling or signs of pain.

8. Listen for any out-of-the-ordinary sounds emanating from your goat. Any wheezing or coughing may indicate body pain being present in the chest or abdomen.

9. Test your animal for blindness. Move your hand toward your goat's eye, but resist the urge to merely fan the air. Even a blind goat will blink if it feels air movement on its face. Instead, move your hand steady and straight toward the suspected eye. Any blinking will indicate that the goat can see.

10. Observe if your animal shows any signs of diarrhea, a runny nose where the discharge appears to be cloudy or clear, crusty eyes, runny eyes, or excessive salivation. Let your vet know what you are noticing.

11. If you are examining a doe, always check her udder and notice if there are any hard knots, heat, clots, or signs of bloody milk. Note if the udder seems painful.

12. A stethoscope should be in your first aid kit because you will be able to use it in the detection of abnormal sounds emanating from the chest or abdomen area. If you do not have a stethoscope, place your ear against the animal's

chest or abdomen and listen, making note of anything you hear.

By keeping detailed notes about your initial examination, you will have a list of symptoms to help you identify what is wrong with your animal or relay those findings to your vet. Having detailed records will help you identify if your animal is improving during treatment. You can utilize a simple spreadsheet to help you keep track of specific readings or information.

Always consult with your veterinarian before administering any treatments, and remember to read all the label instructions for any drug you are using on your animals.

Your animals will need periodic blood tests, vaccinations, and constant observation while you monitor them for any signs or symptoms of health issues.

Disease Descriptions

- **Acidosis** can occur when a goat has eaten too much feed that contains high levels of starch and sugar. This list includes grains, grain by-products, and vegetable parts. Any of these will make the rumen create more acid, giving your goat a stomachache.

  Symptoms are bloat, dehydration, a weak pulse, increased respiration, and appear to be weak. There will be no rumen movement and the stomach will appear full and watery.

  Treatment includes the administering of mineral oil via a stomach tube to help break up any excess gas.

- **Enterotoxemia** is caused by an organism that is found in the intestines of goats, however, when a feeding schedule drastically changes or large amounts of grain are eaten, this will cause the organism to grow rapidly, producing a toxin that can cause death within a few hours.

  Symptoms are a full stomach, a fever, star gazing, convulsions, and tooth grinding. Sudden death is common for this.

  Treatment includes the administration of immediate antitoxin. Prevention is two doses of vaccine.

- **Caprine arthritis-encephalitis (CAE)** is a virus that spreads from an older, infected goat to kids. An example of how this can be spread is from an infected doe to her kid through milk. Even though the testing for this virus yields a high percentage of positive tests, only a small number of animals ever show signs of this disease.

  Symptoms for young goats include becoming weak in the rear legs with progressive weakness until death. Adults will exhibit swollen joints.

  Unfortunately, there are no treatment procedures, and the prevention of this is to test your bloodlines and use culling for any positive stock.

- **Caseous lymphadenitis (CL)** is contracted by consuming a contaminated feed or through an open wound. There is some speculation that this can even enter through unbroken skin. The bacteria that cause this disease is commonly found in soil.

  Symptoms include large knots and abscesses located on the goat's body around their lymph nodes. The animal will start losing its body condition and exhibit a fever.

The treatment is to lance the abscesses and rinse with 7 percent iodine and injectable antibiotics.

- **Chlamydiosis** is one of the causes of reproductive failure in goats. The disease manifests as abortion, stillbirth, and weak kids. Abortion usually manifests during the last 2 to 3 weeks of the doe's gestation and does not necessarily become apparent when the animal was originally infected. It is important to note that this CAN be spread to humans, so caution must be observed.

  Treatment includes antibiotics as advised by your veterinarian. Prevention requires herd testing.

- **Coccidiosis** is caused by a parasite that is found within the cells of a goat's intestines. Depending upon the number of parasites present in the intestines, it can dictate how severe a case may be. If this animal becomes stressed, you will notice the symptoms become worse and lower the animal's resistance to other diseases.

  Symptoms include bloody diarrhea, a loss of appetite, weight, and a possibility of sudden death.

Treatment is the sulfa drug, isolating the sick animal, and good sanitation practices on the property.

- **Flystrike** is fairly rare in goats, as the primary target is typically sheep. This occurs when maggots of blowflies hatch on the skin and feed on the animal's living tissue. This occurs when adult flies lay their eggs in a moistened coat from urine or fecal staining. Skin wounds, weeping eyes, or lesions from footrot can be targeted by the adult flies.

    Symptoms will include agitation, secondary bacterial infections, picking at infected areas, exhibiting a foul smell, and flies targeting one particular animal.

    Treatment for this includes close clipping of affected areas, removing the affected animals from the balance of the herd, cleaning and dressing any area showing infection, and the application of antibiotics at the discretion of your veterinarian.

- **Internal parasites** generally cover the various worms that your goat can be exposed to by grazing in pastures. Each distinct type of worm will have its own lifecycles and can appear at different times of the year. Worms are typically indicated by a decrease in body weight, body muscling, or a loss of appetite.

Symptoms include increased pulse, increased respiration, swelling under the chin area, and severe weakness.

Owners should consult with their veterinarian to determine the most effective dewormer to use. All animals should follow routine deworming practices as well as being dewormed at purchase and when put on any pasture.

- **Pinkeye** is identified by redness and watering in the eye. You may see eyelid swelling or a clouding of the pupil. Besides being transmitted from goat to goat, pinkeye can hop species and even infect humans, so it is important to follow protocols and head off an outbreak to your herd or other animals. Pinkeye will remain contagious for as long as symptoms remain and for a period of 24 hours after administering antibiotics.

Treatment includes injectable antibiotics and the application of eye ointment.

- A **ringworm** is actually not a worm, but instead a skin fungus that looks circular and scaly. This can be caused by unclean conditions or even be found after living dormant in your soil. Consult your vet immediately, as with pinkeye, this can easily hop species and be contracted by humans.

Symptoms include rough circular patches over the body.

Treatment includes consulting with your veterinarian to find the safest treatment available to you.

- **Sore mouth** is a viral disease common in sheep and goats, and the virus that causes it can also lay dormant in your soil or on the surface of barn equipment. Symptoms include thick and scabby sores that are typically found on the lips or gums of the suspected infected animal. If the case is severe enough, you may find these scabs on the udders of does. This condition is very painful and does will be unable to nurse. Always monitor your animal to make sure that they are eating and drinking enough.

  Treatment includes a vaccine for kids and the use of a softening ointment to help with existing sores on the animal's body. Use extreme caution around your goat's eyes.

- **Urinary Calculi** is specific to male goats and is best compared to kidney stones in humans. It is the formation of stones in the male's urinary tract. Calculi is caused by an imbalance of calcium-phosphorus levels found in your feed ratios.

  Symptoms include being unable to pass urine, kicking at the belly, restlessness, and stretching while attempting to urinate.

Treatment involves paying strict attention to your feed ratios. They should have a 2:1 calcium-phosphorus ratio, and 10 t0 15 pounds of ammonium chloride per ton. Following these guidelines and supplying plenty of clean, fresh drinking water will help stop the formation of calculi.

Basic First Aid Supplies

- Thermometers
- Disposable gloves
- Scissors
- Surgical Scissors
- Needles (22g, 20g, 18g)
- Syringes (3cc, 6cc, 10 cc, 20cc)
- Red top tubes. These are used for blood collection for mail-in tests for CAE & CL
- Vet Wrap, elastic bandage
- Gauze Pads
- Cotton Balls
- Alcohol prep wipes
- Triple Antibiotic Ointment
- Vetricyn Spray
- Betadine or Iodine scrub
- Rubbing alcohol
- Terramycin eye ointment
- 7% Iodine solution spray
- Antiseptic spray like Blu-Kote

- Di-Methox powder or liquid for coccidiosis or scours
- Epinephrine, for reactions to injections
- Procaine penicillin
- LA-200 or Biomycin
- Tetanus antitoxin
- Probiotics like Probios
- Powdered electrolytes
- Fortified vitamin B
- CDT antitoxin
- Milk of magnesia for bloat
- Kaolin pectin for scours
- Aspirin
- Activated charcoal product, for example, Toxiban, for accidental poisoning
- Green goo animal formula (for wound care)
- Drench Syringe
- Weight tape
- Scalpels
- Tube-feeding kit to feed sick or weak kids
- Small clippers for shaving wounds
- Blood stop powder or cornstarch
- Children's liquid Benadryl
- Mastitis Test Strips (if you are milking)
- Heat lamps (kidding), heating pad
- Notepad & pen
- Headlamp and flashlight

Conclusion

There are many people out there that are looking to start up their small business on their own land or becoming more self-sufficient. Equally, there is something satisfying about building something with your own two hands.

You may have dreams of starting your own small herd and creating goods from their gifts, such as milk or fiber. If you have never done this before, it may be difficult to navigate how to get started, where to purchase your seed stock, and what animals to choose.

That's why we have put this book together, to help you determine where to get started and why. Besides details about the more popular breeds of goats today, this book addressed detailed questions to ask, information that should be given to you, and how to prepare your property to house your new investment.

Goats are adventurous, and it can be difficult to keep them fenced in because they are such proficient escape artists. The key is to keep them happy on their side of the fence and provide them with a proper and safe environment filled with tasty weeds and shrubbery overgrowth, since those are their favorite snacks.

If you are new to caring for goats, we have given you insight into how to feed them, so they stay healthy and continue producing goods for you.

Dairy goats are probably the most popular herd today, and there is so much more than just getting goat's milk involved with your new venture. This book has given you a small sampling of recipes that you can create using your new homegrown supply, and there are so many more choices out there! We hope that you will enjoy making cheese, ice cream, and more!

If you choose to start a meat goat herd, you now have a list of some of the best breeds to use to solidify your business. It can be difficult getting started, but once you are in the eye of a recurring buyer, you may receive a contract if you continue to improve your herd's confirmation and your reputation for raising the very best animals.

It can be challenging and a bit scary taking that leap and getting started in your chosen goat business. With determination and quality, you will find your niche in the market.

We have explained how important it is to keep records of your venture. This way you will know how much you are spending and how you are improving the bloodlines of your herd.

Another choice, of course, is raising fiber goats. With them, you will enter the world of textiles, and right now, there is more demand than there is production. You received tips on shearing and terminology associated with the industry that will make you sound like a pro.

Lastly, you now have in dept information about keeping your herd healthy and some challenges that you may face. We never want to, but it helps to be prepared for any emergency! Along with those disease descriptions, this book has included a basic first aid kit supply list that you will want to assemble and keep handy.

Raising your own herd will help you become more self-sufficient and teach you about living off the land. They will give you milk to drink, food to eat and provide you with entertainment and companionship.

They can be instrumental in clearing land of unwanted vegetation, they even clear poison ivy!

By reading through all the materials, you can knowledgeably decide which goats are right for you. Happy Herding!

References

Alphafoodie, S. (2020, July 29). *How to make goat cheese (plus FAQs and tips).* Alphafoodie. https://www.alphafoodie.com/how-to-make-goat-cheese/

Analida. (2020, January 7). *How to make goat cheese recipe - Chèvre.* Analida's Ethnic Spoon. https://ethnicspoon.com/how-to-make-goat-cheese-recipe-chevre/

Bradshaw, A. (2015, March 5). *Goats for sale - 6 mistakes to avoid when buying goats.* Common Sense Home. https://commonsensehome.com/goats-for-sale/

Carroll, R. (2018). *Home cheese making : recipes for 75 homemade cheeses.* Storey Books. (Original work published 1982)

Castration | Agricultural Research. (n.d.). www.luresext.edu. Retrieved June 5, 2021, from http://www.luresext.edu/?q=content/castration#:~:text=Three%20common%20ways%20to%20castrate

Fiber Goats – The american goat federation. (n.d.). American goat federation. Retrieved June 8, 2021, from https://americangoatfederation.org/breeds-of-goats-2/fiber-

goats/#:~:text=The%20Fiber%20Goat%20ind
ustry%20has

Garman, J. (2020, January 4). *How long do goats live? - Backyard Goats.* Backyard Goats. https://backyardgoats.iamcountryside.com/hea lth/how-long-do-goats-live/

Griffith, K., Rask, G., Peel, K., Levalley, S., & Johnson, C. (n.d.). *Raising and showing meat goats! A youth manual for meat goat projects in Colorado!* . Retrieved June 8, 2021, from https://www.meadowlark.k-state.edu/docs/4h/resources/Meat_Goat_Man ual.pdf

Harlow, I. (2015, February 13). *Goats for land management.* Farm and Dairy. https://www.farmanddairy.com/top-stories/goats-land-management/240237.html#:~:text=If%20you %20want%20to%20clear

Helmer, J. (2020, December 7). *Tips for providing your goats the shelter they need.* Hobby Farms. https://www.hobbyfarms.com/tips-providing-goats-shelter-they-need/

Kopf, A. : K. (2021, January 19). *Goat lice: are your goats lousy?* Backyard Goats. https://backyardgoats.iamcountryside.com/hea lth/goat-lice-are-your-goats-lousy/

Manteuffel, R. (2019, August 13). *Are goats the new weed whackers? Plenty of people want them to be.* The Washington Post.

https://www.washingtonpost.com/lifestyle/ma
gazine/using-goats-to-clear-land-is-way-more-
labor-intensive-than-anyone-can-
imagine/2019/08/13/acc17608-b78e-11e9-
b3b4-2bb69e8c4e39_story.html

Manuel, A. (n.d.). *How to make goat milk candles.* Home
Guides | SF Gate. Retrieved June 6, 2021, from
https://homeguides.sfgate.com/make-goat-
milk-candles-74284.html

Metzger, M. (2018, December 14). *Winter management tips
for goats.* sheep & goats.
https://www.canr.msu.edu/news/winter-
management-tips-for-
goats#:~:text=Goats%20that%20are%20prope
rly%20cared

*Nutritional feeding management of meat goats | NC State
Extension Publications.* (2015). Ncsu.edu.
https://content.ces.ncsu.edu/nutritional-
feeding-management-of-meat-goats

Nuwer, R. (2014, March 26). *Never underestimate a goat;
it's not as stupid as it looks.* Smithsonian;
Smithsonian.com.
https://www.smithsonianmag.com/science-
nature/never-underestimate-goat-not-stupid-
looks-180950265/

Pesaturo, J. (2014, February 10). *Goat milk ice cream bases
|.* Our One Acre Farm.
https://ouroneacrefarm.com/2014/02/10/goat
-milk-ice-cream-bases/

Ploetz, K. (2013, July 16). *The law | rspca.org.uk.* Rspca.org.uk. https://www.rspca.org.uk/adviceandwelfare/fa rm/farmanimals/goats/law

Poindexter, J. (2017, March 22). *Goat fencing: 6 important tips to consider to build the perfect fence.* MorningChores. https://morningchores.com/goat-fencing/

Roy's Farm. (2021a, May 17). *Raising goats as pets: beginner's guide for raising pet goats.* Roy's Farm. https://www.roysfarm.com/raising-goats-as-pets/

Roy's Farm. (2021b, May 17). *Why do bucks smell so bad: the secrets of the goaty smell.* Roy's Farm. https://www.roysfarm.com/why-do-bucks-smell-so-bad/

Sartell, J. (2018). *Feeding baking soda to your goats.* Mannapro.com. https://www.mannapro.com/homestead/feedi ng-baking-soda-to-your-goats

smallholderhollow. (n.d.). *Dairy goats: full size vs mini goats.* Retrieved May 27, 2021, from http://smallholderhollow.com/dairy-goats-full-size-vs-mini-goats/

Smith, C. (n.d.-a). *Creating a first aid kit for goats.* Dummies. Retrieved June 8, 2021, from https://www.dummies.com/home-garden/hobby-farming/raising-goats/creating-a-first-aid-kit-for-goats/

Smith, C. (n.d.-b). *How and when to shear your goats*. Dummies. Retrieved June 8, 2021, from https://www.dummies.com/home-garden/hobby-farming/raising-goats/how-and-when-to-shear-your-goats/

Smith, C. (n.d.-c). *What is normal goat behavior?* Dummies. Retrieved May 31, 2021, from https://www.dummies.com/home-garden/hobby-farming/raising-goats/what-is-normal-goat-behavior/

The Hay Manager. (2018, October 31). *Keeping goats warm in the winter*. The Hay Manager. https://www.thehaymanager.com/goat-and-sheep-round-bale-hay-feeders/keeping-goats-warm-in-the-winter/

The Law | rspca.org.uk. (2017). Rspca.org.uk. https://www.rspca.org.uk/adviceandwelfare/farm/farmanimals/goats/law

Tilley, N. (n.d.). *StackPath*. Www.gardeningknowhow.com. Retrieved June 4, 2021, from https://www.gardeningknowhow.com/composting/manures/goat-manure-fertilizer.htm#:~:text=Goat%20manure%20is%20virtually%20odorless

Treehugger. (n.d.). *Learn how to feed and tend goats on the small farm*. Treehugger. Retrieved June 1, 2021, from https://www.treehugger.com/feed-and-tend-goats-

3016793#:~:text=Hay%20is%20the%20main%20source

Vet, S. C. (2019, February 11). *Three diseases all goats owners should be aware of, test for, and work to prevent.* Sale Creek. https://salecreek.vet/three-diseases-all-goats-owners-should-be-aware-of-test-for-and-work-to-prevent/

Wetherbee, K. (n.d.). *Raising dairy goats and the benefits of goat milk.* Mother Earth News. Retrieved June 2, 2021, from https://www.motherearthnews.com/homesteading-and-livestock/benefits-of-goat-milk-zmaz02jjzgoe

Wikipedia Contributors. (2019a, February 27). *Cashmere goat.* Wikipedia; Wikimedia Foundation. https://en.wikipedia.org/wiki/Cashmere_goat

Wikipedia Contributors. (2019b, October 27). *List of goat milk cheeses.* Wikipedia; Wikimedia Foundation. https://en.wikipedia.org/wiki/List_of_goat_milk_cheeses

Wolford, D. (2014a, February 16). *Homemade udder & teat wipes.* Weed 'Em & Reap. https://www.weedemandreap.com/homemade-udder-teat-wipes-milking/

Wolford, D. (2014b, April 5). *How to milk a goat: step by step pictures.* Weed 'Em & Reap. https://www.weedemandreap.com/how-to-milk-a-goat/

Wolford, D. (2016, April 27). *Homemade udder balm recipe {with free printable label}*. Weed 'Em & Reap. https://www.weedemandreap.com/homemade-udder-balm-recipe/

Wright, A. (2013, September 18). *No, goats do not eat tin cans.* Modern Farmer. https://modernfarmer.com/2013/09/goats-eat-tin-cans/#:~:text=They%20can%20be%20pets%2C%20they

www.ingramcontent.com/pod-product-compliance
Lightning Source LLC
Chambersburg PA
CBHW071259310326
41914CB00109B/663